LONG LIVE THE *DELTA QUEEN*

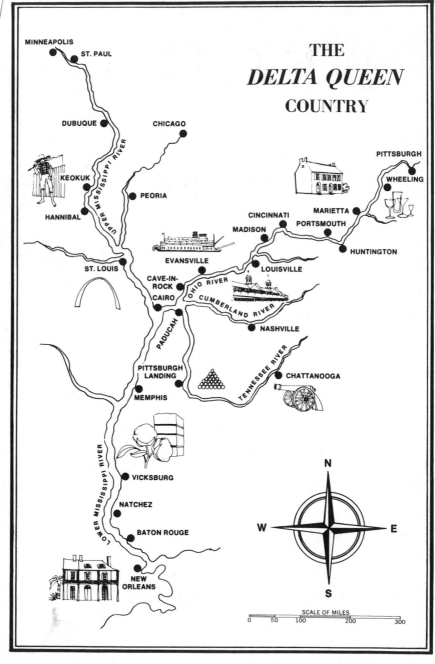

THE *DELTA QUEEN* COUNTRY

MINNEAPOLIS
ST. PAUL
DUBUQUE
CHICAGO
KEOKUK
PEORIA
HANNIBAL
UPPER MISSISSIPPI RIVER
PITTSBURGH
WHEELING
MARIETTA
CINCINNATI
PORTSMOUTH
MADISON
HUNTINGTON
ST. LOUIS
EVANSVILLE
LOUISVILLE
CAVE-IN-ROCK
OHIO RIVER
CAIRO
CUMBERLAND RIVER
PADUCAH
NASHVILLE
TENNESSEE RIVER
PITTSBURGH LANDING
CHATTANOOGA
MEMPHIS
LOWER MISSISSIPPI RIVER
VICKSBURG
NATCHEZ
BATON ROUGE
NEW ORLEANS

N
W   E
S

SCALE OF MILES
0   50   100   200   300

LONG LIVE
the
DELTA QUEEN.

by

LETHA C. GREENE

Illustrated by Tom Greene, Jr.

HASTINGS HOUSE PUBLISHERS

NEW YORK

Second Printing, May 1973

Library of Congress Cataloging in Publication Data

Greene, Letha C
Long live the Delta Queen.

1. Delta Queen (Steamboat) I. Title.
VM461.5.D4G7   386'.22'43   72-13746
ISBN 0-8038-4286-4

PUBLISHED SIMULTANEOUSLY IN CANADA BY
SAUNDERS OF TORONTO, LTD., DON MILLS, ONTARIO

PRINTED IN THE UNITED STATES OF AMERICA

CONTENTS

Introduction and Dedication

A HOUSEWIFE and mother of four, I inherited the duties of managing the steamboat *Delta Queen,* following the death of my forty-six-year-old husband, "Captain Tom", in 1950. A captain and pilot on the Ohio River, he was president of this family-owned business, which his father, Captain Gordon Greene, established in 1890. Of a fleet of twenty-six boats, the *Delta Queen* is the only one remaining, and my book deals with the years I knew, owned, and managed her, until I sold my interests and retired in 1969.

Many friends and passengers from all parts of the country who have travelled on the *Queen,* have urged me to write about my experiences. One of them said the way to do it was, "Just start writing." I hope you may enjoy my efforts in sharing with you some of my river experiences with the *Queen,* the boat of my husband's dream, to which he devoted his life. I dedicate these pages to his fond memory.

The *Queen* has had nation-wide publicity during her five-year congressional battle for existence, but this book shows a little of the day-to-day life on the river, the great crises and the odd incidents, and the happy times enjoyed by those of us who knew her personally. She is still in operation, with a thriving business of people who want to escape today's hectic pace and take a "sentimental journey."

LONG LIVE THE *DELTA QUEEN*

: 1 :

NOSTALGIA

I HAVE WITNESSED her death and rebirth five times. This time, on October 12, 1970, I thought it was final as I stood on the levee at Cincinnati and watched the *Delta Queen* pull out for her last cruise. I was certain I'd purged her out of my system, having directed my interests and energies to other channels, and would never give much further thought to the river and boats. Except in dreams or maybe nightmares.

But there I stood on feet of clay. The life of which I had been so much a part for forty years was sentenced by Congress to end. Steamboat passenger service on the Ohio and Mississippi rivers would be no more, after this final cruise. There was the usual fuss and flurry of sailing day on board, with bon voyage parties, great droves of visitors, photographers snapping parting shots of the *Queen* for their scrapbooks, and newsmen buzzing around with their interviews.

I politely declined invitations to join various groups, to drink and be merry, or perhaps not so merry. As for me, there hung over all an unseen veil of nostalgic memories, some sad, others glad, but all setting me apart in my emotions from the hundreds of other sightseers that day. I preferred to stroll over the boat alone.

I found myself automatically checking, as I had done many times before, when the boat was under my ownership, to be sure the floors were immaculate, deck railings free of soot, or that used mops had not been carelessly left in conspicuous places. I wandered back through the main cabin toward the stern of the boat and stood there alone with my thoughts, watching the big red paddle wheel turn slowly as she warmed up for the eighteen revolutions per minute which would propel the boat down the Ohio and up the Mississippi to St. Paul and then down to New Orleans by November second. November second was the date when high authorities decreed she must close her doors to the type of passengers she had carried for twenty-three years. She would then hang her head and hope for an angel to help her pass her retirement years in some yet unknown type of river service somewhere. All of us, the *Delta Queen,* and her thousands of friends resented the indignity of this forced retirement.

As I walked slowly past the corner parlor I paused. On a fateful sultry July morning in 1950 my husband Captain Tom Greene had suffered his fatal heart attack there. That tragic event changed the lives of so many, and the fate of the *Queen* herself. My son, Tom Jr., once said, "Whatever we are in our family, we are because of the influence of the boats and the river." Perhaps he's right.

I went on down the back stairs and through the dining room, where I greeted the waiters who were busily preparing a delectable buffet luncheon for the one hundred and ninety hungry passengers who would soon be sailing on this last cruise. Every place I went evoked memories. Soon my reverie was broken by an announcement over the public address system: "All ashore that's going ashore", it said authoritatively, "The *Delta Queen* is preparing to leave Cincinnati." On out through the main deck and across the gangplank I walked, waving an apparently cheery farewell to the crowd, keeping my real feelings to myself.

A dignified Roman Catholic priest greeted me as I stepped off the end of the gangplank. I replied, "Hi, Alvin," for I never could bring myself to call him Father Zugelter. Many years ago as a youth he had been an employee of one of our boats. As we stood together sharing an umbrella and watching the boat pull away, tears were in the eyes of everyone around us. Even the sky sent a shower as if grieving at the *Queen's* fate.

The lines were cast off. The *Queen* blew a short final blast of her whistle, backed out, and headed downstream. A band played "Auld Lang Syne" and then the calliope on the stern of the boat took over with "Beautiful Ohio," and "Away Down Yonder in New Orleans." As the *Queen* disappeared from sight, beyond the bridge, I could hear the farewell strains of "When the Saints Go Marching In." That was my husband's favorite river tune, and I somehow believe he was listening. He always had a hand in the shaping of things.

If it had not been for him, there would not have been a *Delta Queen* here today. Captain Tom Greene brought her back to life the first time in 1946, and introduced her to the Ohio River.

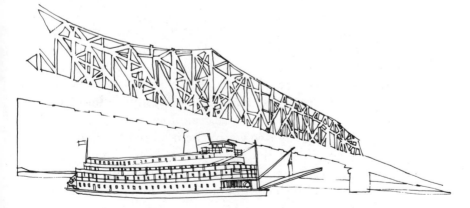

: 2 :   A BID FOR THE QUEEN

MY HUSBAND, Captain Tom Greene, at age twenty-three was master of the packet boat which bore his name and which operated in a passenger and freight business, along with her sister ship the *Chris Greene,* on the Ohio and Kanawha Rivers, but later between Cincinnati, Ohio and Louisville, Kentucky. Greene Line Steamers, which was founded by his father, Captain Gordon C. Greene, in 1890, has owned and operated twenty-six steamboats, and the *Delta Queen* is the last of this fleet in existence today. All of the Greene Line boats were packet boats, carrying both freight and passengers, except the *Gordon C. Greene* and the *Delta Queen.* These two boats operated on a regular schedule the navigable length of the Mississippi, Ohio, Tennessee, Cumberland and Kanawha Rivers, carrying passengers from all over the world on cruises from three days to three weeks in length.

It was in 1935 that the *Gordon C. Greene* was added to the fleet and three years later she extended her passenger service to the Mississippi River, with a cruise to the Mardi Gras in New Orleans. Since the *Gordon* was a smaller, old-fashioned steamboat, with a minimum of free board, she often gave her crew anxious moments in the strong winds and high waves of the mighty turbulent Mississippi. Tom feared that an equinox storm might someday hit. In combination with flood waters, it might be more than the old gal could handle. An angry black funnel cloud dipping from the sky in the middle of Lake Peppin on the run to St. Paul would be cause for any river pilot to say his prayers. Tom was extremely receptive to the idea of owning a sound, more-than-safe boat for the sake of his passengers on the river. And the *Delta Queen* seemed to qualify.

Her triple-galvanized steel hull was fabricated in Scotland on the River Clyde in 1926, assembled, then disassembled. In separate, marked pieces it was then shipped to Stockton, California where it was reassembled and a superstructure added which made her the acme of river steamboats in the United States. The floor of the main deck was of iron bark, an extremely hard, durable wood from what was at that time Siam. Her railings were teakwood, Oregon cedar finished off her cabin deck, and her machinery was a product of Krupp Iron Works in Germany. Truly she was a Queen, as she and her "brother" ship, the *Delta King,* plied the Sacramento River. Her overnight passenger service between San Francisco and Sacramento was interrupted by World War II, when the Navy used her to transport the servicemen to their ships at sea in the Oakland-San Francisco Bay.

The conclusion of our many friends who had travelled these two boats on the Sacramento seemed to be, "Tom, you should have those Delta boats over here on the Ohio and Mississippi. They'd be just right for your purpose."

Tom listened with an open mind, and dreamed. A thought planted in one's mind is very often the seed of things to come. If an idea keeps returning over and over, I have found it's more than likely to become a reality, regardless of cost. But perhaps Tom needed just a little shove in the right direction.

This final shove was probably furnished by a knowledgeable boat-minded businessman from Pasadena, California who made a trip on the *Gordon C. Greene* to New Orleans. He pointed out to Tom how the *King* and *Queen* had been well tried and tested in the San Francisco Bay during their military service. They had handled well any angry billows a Pacific gale could whip up. This Californian could almost see the two boats riding high and safe in the deep swirling waters of the New Orleans harbor, or tied up alongside the many other ships docked there, ships carrying flags from every port of the world.

His words to Tom on that Mississippi cruise aboard the *Gordon C. Greene* fell on fertile ground and produced fruit. One hot summer day in 1946 Tom came home from the river, walked into the kitchen, and paced the floor nervously, shedding his coat, loosening his tie, and opening his shirt collar as he asked me how I'd like to go to California.

I almost dropped the steaks as I slid them onto the sizzling broiler. I was afraid I hadn't heard right. Finally I stammered, "Why, what's that all about, of course I'd love to go to California." It seemed to me any housewife and mother of four active children would be fit for commitment if she didn't jump at the chance.

"Well, you know, I think we should really take a look at those Delta boats. Even if nothing comes of it, we can have a hell of a good vacation," he smiled half guiltily.

The wheels in my own mind clicked into gear: Who'll take care of the children?—Oh, Aunt Vina will help, I know, and I can get outside help too. . . . The older ones are in school. . . . I have my new knitted suits, just right for travelling; San Francisco is cool—But oh, another boat? We already have three, we must be practical. But the high waves of the Mississippi. . . . Oh, well, we probably won't get it.—Who'll fill in for Tom on the Labor Day trip coming up? Our old friend Captain Stogie White could maybe take over. . . . My heart skipped a beat and my face flushed as I called a little louder than usual, "Everyone ready for dinner!"

The following Monday before Labor Day, we loaded our luggage into a cab in front of our home, waved good-bye to the family and both blurted at once, "Union Terminal." There we were joined by our steamboat engineer friend George Wise and were soon ticketed up for a round trip to San Francisco by way of Chicago.

After a smooth but exciting ride over the plains and scenic areas of the Union Pacific domain, we arrived in a misty early morning fog at Oakland, California. From there a ferry boat soon deposited us safely in San Francisco. After we were settled down at the commodious Clift Hotel, we lit out by special limousine for Martinez to look over the boats of our dreams. I entertained myself that first afternoon by watching the fishermen along the dock as they hauled in their catch for the day.

No women were allowed on the little cruiser that provided transportation up to Suisun Bay, where the *King* and *Queen* reposed in their grey death row, along with dozens of other U. S. Navy ships left lonely and unwanted after the smoke and fury of World War II. It's funny how little unimportant incidents will stamp indelibly on the mind: I remember how I searched in vain for a button lost from my brand new suit—darn it, I must get a whole new set now, could never match it up. . . .

It was not until I had signed significant, ominous documents which in essence assured the port authorities that if I broke a leg or fell in the bay, it would be strictly my own fault and responsibility, that I got permission to join the men in taking a look at the *Queen*. It was fun, though, cutting out across the wide Suisun Bay in the little grey cruiser out of which I scrambled and pulled my way up over the high, wide, sturdy freeboard decks of the *Queen*.

Tom and George measured, figured, discussed machinery, and scanned her from stem to stern for five days. I was vastly more interested in her décor potential, and the appointments of her staterooms, her beautiful grand staircase, and other things a woman would naturally appreciate. We all talked *Delta Queen* during daylight hours and well into the night, always looking for "the crack in the wall." Would she suit our needs? Would it be a wise investment? So much remodeling would have to be done. . . . But the most important fact was that she was built like a superdreadnaught and was seaworthy.

There were many other pluses, but many minuses were yet to be discovered. Still, the seed was planted and a real Banyan Tree was to result.

We returned home by way of the Feather River Route, which was more scenic, less luxurious, but much more fun. The post-war travellers filled the diner to capacity on Sunday night, so we decided to wait until after the place cleared out to enjoy a leisurely dinner in more privacy. At Salt Lake City, to our great disappointment, the diner was taken off. There was no chance of a warm meal, and the salted peanuts we shared from a tin can George opened with his pocket knife tasted to us like pheasant under glass at the Waldorf.

Our spirits were further improved later by the porter's announcement as he came down the aisle, "Ham or cheese sandwiches, coffee. Ham or cheese sandwiches, coffee." He went no further in his monotone announcement, for all the hungry passengers soon cleaned out his supply and sent him scurrying for more. We were not the only ones who had missed our dinner.

Following our arrival back in Cincinnati, many meetings and conferences were held with officials and advisors of Greene Line. They were anxious to hear Tom's report. We were quite aware of the restricted budget for expansion, and we were not unaware of the need for a better boat. Should we make a bid for her? I am reminded that my professor in political science once advanced the idea that any decision one carries out is the result of forces so strong that it could never have been any other way. Since factors were strong for Greene Line procuring the *Delta Queen,* perhaps it couldn't have been any other way.

When Tom phoned me from the wharf boat office one afternoon to tell me of his luck in being the only bidder for the *Queen,* I replied, "Send them back a telegram saying, 'Forget the whole thing, we were just kidding.' "

The *Queen* was Greene Line property on the west coast, and we were on the Ohio River. Had we opened a Pandora's Box? After the first shock, the warm thrill of ownership came over us: Yes, she'd be safer, and would carry many more passengers in her rooms, which were equipped with private baths. She'd be fun to remodel and redecorate. And so many of the minus factors slowly gave way to enthusiastic anticipation. The astrologers would have said we were about to enter a new plateau of our lives, one which would also affect the lives of thousands of the travelling public.

: 3 :

THE QUEEN IS RELUCTANT

CAPTAIN TOM GREENE entrusted the Greene Line coffers, almost without reservation to our good river and writer friend, Captain Fred Way, Jr.

"Fred, go out there and get the *Queen* ready to come around to these parts. Spend what it takes, ride her around if you want to—you'll get enough experience for another book. And we'll have the finest boat to offer these river fans that has ever been dreamed up around here. Remember though, if things get too rough or dangerous, think only of the safety of yourself and your men, and to hell with the boat."

A crew of Greene Line men led by Captain Way started for the West Coast and big adventure. It was necessary for Tom to remain in Cincinnati and look after the business. This meant keeping the *Gordon* in operation, for after all she was the money maker at that time. The *Tom* and the *Chris* were also part of the fleet, and there was much responsibility at home.

At Fulton Shipyards in Antioch, California the *Delta Queen* was crated up to protect her from the ocean waves, her wheel was removed, and great tarpaulins were tightly secured over the smokestacks in preparation for her voyage around to New Orleans. An ocean tug named the *Osage* was engaged to tow the *Queen* on this thirty-day voyage. Our first financial blow came when the union crew of the *Osage* was not permitted to deal with our non-union

Greene Line men. No, they would not splash a salty wave until the *Queen* was fully outfitted with a crew of ten, including a captain, mates, deck hands and all, almost as if she were an in-service boat. The larder had to be equipped with plenty of proper food to satisfy their appetities for the lengthy trip. This unexpected setback cost Greene Line $10,000 before the boat ever left California.

It seemed a bit ominous that the *Queen* appeared reluctant to leave her home state, and she demanded front and center attention from the start. During the process of her being bridled onto the *Osage,* she was caught by a strong gale, turned around and jammed into a mud bank of the Sacramento River. There she stuck long enough to make headlines in newspapers across the country before settling down, willing to be led docilely out of the river and out into the wide Pacific Ocean.

She tossed, bucked and plunged in the severe storms off the coast of Mexico, listing to a 26° angle. But she always righted herself, which proved her seaworthiness to our satisfaction. We would have been less than sad, however, if her crew were green around the gills from seasickness.

For weeks we anxiously awaited news of the boat's safe arrival in New Orleans. A Greene Line crew was alerted to meet her there, where she would shed her wooden crating and get her machinery in order to come upstream under her own steam. Now the crew would be composed of our own employees plus a few extras thrown in. Many of Tom's business friends said hopefully, "Tom, can you use an extra deck hand? I have an awful urge to ride that boat up from New Orleans on her first trip on the Mississippi River."

Tom always enjoyed fun, and where possible loved to mix it in proper proportions with business. So he corralled a number of his business friends in the area of Cincinnati

and Louisville and invited them to pack a few old clothes
and meet the boat at Harvey Canal in New Orleans when
the *Queen* arrived. They could help out on deck, handle
the lines, go barefoot, grow a beard, fish, or do whatever
they pleased when off duty. The engineer's wife would pre-
pare the meals and ten days of this beachcomber life
would be therapy for frayed nerves and high blood pressure. This odd working vacation would refresh the minds
and bodies of all these business and professional men, and
they all accepted the offer to have the first ride on the only
steamboat ever to go through the Panama Canal.

: 4 :   DEBITS

THE PHONE RANG. It was Tom, "Letha, pack a bag for me.
The *Delta Queen* has reached New Orleans and I'll have
to leave on the next train. That crew want to be returned
to California by air. Can't wait, it looks like."

"Well, what do you know! I guess you'll need plenty
of work clothes, as well as some good ones. You'll be up at
the Harvey Canal, won't you?"

"Yes. And, say, fix old Gordon up to make the trip too
—this is one he'll remember. He should go along and ride
up from New Orleans."

Gordon was ecstatic and started hunting for his fishing rod and reel, and many other bulky toys which had to
be eliminated for this overnight train ride. I immediately
became the mother hen, thinking of so many risks for a
boy of twelve: He'll get filthy dirty there without Aunt
Vina or me to get after him . . . he may get homesick.
. . . But at the same time I searched for his oldest
clothes and cleaned his gym shoes of the mud from his
last baseball game, hoping he'd survive this adventure.

But this was a special occasion, and worth the risk.
The next evening, excited and happy, they both waved
goodbye from the window of the departing *L & N Hum-
mingbird* train. I had my fingers crossed, though.

The following weeks in New Orleans were romantic,
adventurous ones with this friendly crew of the *Delta
Queen*. Mosquitoes were rife at the Canal and the weather

23

was hot. Dan Startsman declared he overheard two mosquitoes holding a conference on the foot of his bed, "We'd better eat him here. If we take him down to the water's edge the big ones will take him away from us." The second mosquito concurred.

Everyone resembled smallpox victims as a result of the unabated attack of these pests, which seemed to thrive on insecticide as a cat responds to catnip. There was much work to be done, but the wonderful French restaurants in New Orleans offered respite and a good cause for donning city clothes when it became necessary to take a few hours vacation.

I anxiously awaited news from the boat. At last it came, "The *Delta Queen* will arrive in Louisville Saturday night. Bring the kids and come down to meet us. Signed, Tom."

I never heard a whistle sound so pretty as when she first blew for the landing at Louisville. As we glided so smoothly upstream it was like floating on a mysterious magic carpet. No sensation of moving, or of the waves rocking. I could realize the boat was in motion only by observing the changing shoreline as it slowly slipped by. There was no noise of the wheel and machinery compared with the *Gordon* or the *Tom*. The *Queen* was heavy in the water, no question there.

Our son Gordon was the dirtiest twelve-year-old I'd ever seen. He couldn't wait to show me the pump he and Jim Way had been working on, and then he led me up to his sleeping quarters: two mattresses piled on the bare floor of a room on top deck. Huckleberry Finn would have been envious.

Those sailors in San Francisco Bay had given the *Queen* some pretty discourteous treatment. The beds were not in any good order, knife throwing contests had been aimed at many of the wooden bulkheads, and since something was definitely unright with the oil burners the smoke had boiled down over the decks uncontrollably, all the way up the river.

The Oregon cedar bulkheads gave the entire boat an aroma I'd never encountered before. Perfumes can do funny things to a person at times. Even today whenever the carpenter has reason to saw through a bit of this woodwork for any remodeling, a strong fragrance is released. It brings me nostalgic memories of misty fog in the night, wet drooping willow branches, peaceful sunny afternoons, color-splashed sunsets, landing whistles, the clang of engine room bells and the bumping of lock walls. And I would hear again a welcome dinner gong, brisk organ music, smell the tempting aroma of broiling steaks, hear the splashing of the paddle wheel or watch with awe the swollen flood waters—all these things a part of the *Delta Queen*. The woodwork itself, however, was to get her into serious conflict with Senators one day.

After arrival in Cincinnati, the *Queen* was detained only a few days before being detailed to Dravo Shipyard in Pittsburgh. This was the genesis of a long relationship with that place of business, inasmuch as it was the only shipyard in the upper Ohio of adequate size to drydock the 285-foot-long *Delta Queen*.

Since the boat was going upstream, since my sister Leoma, whom we planned to visit, lived in eastern Pennsylvania, and since it was cheaper to ride the boat than to pay train fare, we rode the *Delta Queen* as far as Pittsburgh when she went to dry dock. Many varieties of clothing had to be packed: old clothes for the boat, and city duds for the trip on east. The smoke situation had not appreciably improved, and the decks were still black from the billowing smoke. My dear sister Vina, who was along and who believed that cleanliness was next to, if not equal to godliness, personally wielded a ten-pound mop over the decks in a futile attempt to keep them clean, at least immediately outside our rooms. I gave up before I began, for I saw it was impossible to lick the situation. I figured that when we arrived in Pittsburgh we could take off to a hotel, where baths could be enjoyed every hour on the hour if necessary. But until such time it was, "Relax and don't worry, everyone will wash up without fading."

Young and full of dreams, I was still in awe of the new boat and its potential. The fun we'd have decorating! What a great family project!

The boat remained at Dravo Shipyards for her face lifting for nearly nine months. As we all learned, shipyard work doesn't come cheap. A set amount was budgeted for the remodeling of the *Delta Queen,* but right there we learned that any estimate one may make regarding building or remodeling, be it ship, boat or home must be mentally doubled or at least one third added in order to be realistic. The first bill we received from the shipyard was over half the total amount budgeted for the entire work, and scarcely anything had been done. I'll never forget one morning Tom returned from Pittsburgh on the night train. I opened the door at six o'clock in the morning and thought he'd had a seizure. When he showed me the first bill, we both wept.

From this time on it was a matter of dollars, and how best to handle this monster we had turned loose on the gentle, peaceful Greene Line fold. In September of that year the *Island Queen* of the Coney Island Company met disaster and we thought the *Delta Queen* just might be the answer to their sudden need. We approached President Ed Schott about this possibility, and he seemed interested. So we were hopeful.

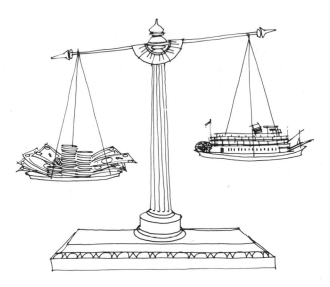

At the Taft Hotel in New York, a telegram was delivered to our room, and I feared one of the children might have been run down by a car or something. This fear was assuaged but the telegram was still bad news: "Have looked into the *Delta Queen*. Not suitable for our purpose. Ed Schott." We started on our trek next morning in quest of furnishings for the boat: she was all ours.

The following months were a montage of trips to Pittsburgh and decisions, decisions: how to finance this project, and generally—what to do? Honesty was a key word in Greene Line company policy and we had been schooled not to overspend or incur debts beyond what one could foresee as legitimate income. The Greenes never operated on bluffs or false promises.

New rooms were added, air conditioning installed, new decks built, and much done that I, as a woman, don't even yet comprehend. There were lengthy conferences at the bank, and many anxious and trying times. This, however, was just the beginning of what the *Delta Queen* had brought with her. She trailed not Wordsworth's clouds of glory, but clouds of gloom and tragedy along with the romance, joy, and pleasure we had dreamed of. What was the strange pull of this crate of steel and wood that would impel me to face Columbia Parkway's eight o'clock chariot race in order to witness her return to life in the Cincinnati harbor over twenty years later? Did she have demonic powers, this thing that had brought so much to our family on the debit side of the ledger, yet drew us to her like a moth to a flame? Too bad business adventures cannot be evaluated in terms of romantic standards. If so, we could perhaps still drive safely to town in a horse-drawn buggy, or maybe a fortune could be realized in the manufacture of hoop skirts. Maybe investments in an ox-bow factory might raise the Dow-Jones average. But no matter how glamorous a business may seem to the layman, underneath the exterior padding lies that skeleton of iron and teeth: Will it pay off?

Our good friends at the bank came to our rescue and enabled us to finance our project, but with a heavy mortgage which burdened the company for many years.

: 5 : THE MAIDEN VOYAGE

Two days after the *Delta Queen* docked in Cincinnati, the *Gordon C. Greene* was scheduled to arrive there at midnight with a full complement of passengers from a trip to Charleston and Marietta. As the *Gordon's* guests were eager to have a look at the new *Delta Queen,* all accepted Captain Tom's invitation to come aboard. Captain Mary Greene, my husband's mother, led the crowd out of the *Gordon* across the wharf boat and down to the exit opening onto the *Queen's* deck. Everyone respectfully stood aside to allow Captain Mary to be the first to cross the threshold of the newest addition to her fleet, in deference to her acknowledged priority in river circles.

Captain Mary had learned the river under the capable guidance of her husband, Captain Gordon Greene, when she came as a bride to that first Greene Line boat, the *H. K. Bedford,* in 1890. After her husband's death in 1927, as the matriarch of the company and a captain and pilot in her own right, she had led her two captain sons Tom and Chris in the responsibility of carrying on the business. The business grew, and at all times her opinion and advice were highly respected. Not many moves were made without her full blessing.

Tom said, "Mom, I've got the best room on the boat picked out for you, and you'll love the private bath it has. You'll have a chance to live in a little more luxury on the river now."

I never felt that Captain Mary fully transferred her deep affection from the *Gordon C.* to the *Delta Queen,* for she seemed to be more at home on the smaller Mark Twain type of boat with which she was more familiar. Nevertheless, as was befitting her outgoing personality, she adapted well to the new surroundings and lived on the boat during the tourist season until her death one year after the *Queen's* maiden voyage. Captain Mary loved people, and was happiest when her steamboat guests were happy and getting what she considered their money's worth, and when things were running smoothly. In spite of her advanced age, she still reigned supreme with her zestful, vibrant personality until the very last of her eighty-first year.

It was on the *Queen's* maiden voyage that a couple approached the purser and the wife spoke up, "Mr. McCann, we're back in Room 101 and I noticed a man and wife in Parlor B leave the boat back at the last town. Now can't we just move in there? We're a little crowded in our space and I know the folder shows that room to have twin beds and more room."

"Certainly, lady, providing, of course, you pay the difference in fare. You see, that Parlor B carries a higher rate than Room 101."

"Well, I just don't think I want to pay more, but I can't see why we can't move in—it's empty," she reasoned.

"Yes, I know, but we have to go by I.C.C. rules and regulations and I can't let you have Parlor B unless you pay the fare it calls for," he explained.

"Well, I'm going to see Captain Mary about this. I know she'll do something about it. She'll understand," And with those words she started looking around for Captain Mary, to present her case.

Later, I heard, "Bob, that lady wants Parlor B so bad

and she's pestering me so. Just let her have it. No one is going to use it."

"No, Captain Mary, if I do that, she'll tell everyone on this boat and we'll never hear the end of it. Besides, it's against the law. If she wants it she'll just have to pay the difference."

Much, much later: "Bob, look, I'll pay the difference on that room. I'll give you a check myself, just to get that woman satisfied. She's been to me four times."

"Captain Mary, that's an imposition on you, and I'll not let you do it. She's unreasonable, and for once I'll not obey orders."

Even though Mrs. Bostwick didn't get her Parlor B, she and her husband made from one to three cruises every year as long as they both lived. And she came alone later, as a widow. I'm sure her contribution to the Green Line till would run into a fat five figures over the years. She loved the boat and was a friend of Greene Line for all of her remaining life.

This maiden voyage was quite a shakedown experience. In fact, the first few years were very nearly a continuous shakedown until we finally got things in fine shape— after we really got acquainted with the *Queen*.

I found that getting her ready for a first cruise was a stupendous job in areas where I fit in as well as the engineer's department, culinary department or pilot house. In a moment of weakness, I volunteered to sew every drape that adorned her three decks, in order to save much-needed funds. And I had nightmares of being surrounded by Singer sewing machines that turned into gigantic steel monsters, equipped with titanic paddle wheels threatening my extinction as they splashed after me with large bolts of flowered linen draped from their needle-like teeth.

By the time we got around to considering buying a

piano, we all took a long look at our Baldwin baby grand that sat in our own Hyde Park living room. The Company's funds were low, so I gave the baby a fond pat as I resigned her to her public life in the dining room of the *Delta Queen,* where cigarette butts and alcohol rings would be sure to mar her satin-smooth mahogany finish, or a careless beer-drinker would drench her delicate innards. She's on the boat today, in good tune and in daily use. After a taste of colorful river life she never returned home.

The smoke continued to be a hellish problem until expensive new burners were installed. And then there was the unholy tiller line, a demon of steel wire cable extending from pilot wheel to the rudders. It was temperamental and broke frequently, leaving the direction of the boat to sheer luck and manpower until repairs could be made. A new hydraulic system was then installed which eliminated one "bug" at least.

The newly-constructed front parlors on cabin deck did not receive cool air as theorized by authorities. The purser was faced with the challenge of explaining the unfortunate situation in devious ways to the occupants of these areas on every hot summer trip. Law suits were threatened and customers screamed, "false advertising!" I couldn't blame them, but there was nothing we could do that first year. Today the problem doesn't exist, and many of the good passengers will not travel if they can not be assigned to their favorite room: one of these cabin deck parlors.

On the first cruises of the *Delta Queen* the crew ate in the cook house in the hold of the boat, where the temperature was uncontrollably hot. How we'd gnaw through our fresh roasting ears and tender roast beef, swallow our ice cream so fast it would almost freeze our gullets, then hurry upstairs to cool off! Later we graduated to the main dining room, where long tables for the crew were set up in the ell-shaped corners of the stern end of this big room, away from passengers but yet in full view of them all.

My ten-year-old son Tom was not allowed to drink coffee, but occasionally he'd indulge in this forbidden sin when aboard the boat. This day he ate his meal with great anticipation of the precious cup of half coffee and half milk by his plate.

Close by sat a lady passenger whom he knew he'd confront as his teacher at the next session of Hyde Park School. His guilt complex assured him she was watching his every move, when in reality she was scarcely aware that he was on board. From the corner of his eye he watched until he felt sure she had her face turned toward the outside window to view the scenery. He grabbed his coffee cup and muttering to himself, "Here's my chance," gulped it down.

Similar sensitive moments were eliminated when those two ell-shaped areas were later partitioned off, decorated by mirrors from other dismantled boats, and bordered by iron scroll work. The port section became the crew's dining room and the starboard became a cocktail lounge, privately partitioned off from the huge Orleans Room, as the dining room was later called.

Those were the precious pioneer days. Passengers who travel today, twenty-three years later on the *Delta Queen* with her wall-to-wall carpeting, fireproof paint, new electrically equipped kitchen and modern safety features would find the earlier circumstances hard to believe. Yes, everything known to the marine world has been done for the comfort of all who choose a restful, rare and historic vacation aboard the *Delta Queen*.

6

PADUCAH AND
KENTUCKY LAKE

FOR MANY YEARS the summer schedule of the *Delta Queen* consisted of regular seven-day cruises to Kentucky Lake on the Tennessee River. The boat left Cincinnati each Saturday evening at eight and returned the following Friday around midnight. Passengers could remain aboard and leave on Saturday morning after breakfast. A fast clean-up job aboard the boat and replenishment of supplies enabled us to start registration of new passengers by six Saturday evening. The new crowd usually arrived at the boat hot, tired and somewhat puzzled about their new environment: we weren't the *Ile De France* or the *Queen Mary*. The accommodations were deluxe as far as river steamboats went, but some passengers seemed to expect more than they found.

Housewives had brought with them thoughts of, "Oh, did I leave the iron turned on?" Or, "I wonder how Fido will get along in the kennel while I'm gone." Or, "Oh how I hated to leave the baby with Grandma, I hope it won't be too much for her to look after." Men would have come straight from the rat race of the business world, carrying on at the same momentum and unable to unwind all at once. Directions and locations aboard the boat were confusing for the first few hours.

The purser was assailed by many questions: "Do I go up the stairs to get to the top deck?", "What time do we arrive in St. Louis?" and one lady even inquired, "When do we stop in Kansas City?" It must have been a strange world to our landlubber guests.

If I was not aboard the boat for the entire trip, I always tried to get on for this first night to see the cruise off as far as Louisville. The hostess always planned a short welcome address to the guests and a healthy buffet was served after leaving port at eight o'clock. I have returned home from Louisville on Sunday morning almost every way except thumbing a ride. I knew the exact bus schedules, train schedules, plane flights and often times I would put my car aboard the *Queen* so I could drive home. The following Friday morning I would travel to Madison, a distance of some sixty-five miles where the boat docked for a conducted tour of that charming Indiana town.

I then came upstream on the last day of the trip, arriving in Cincinnati around midnight. I could talk with the passengers and see how they enjoyed the trip, check on other things pertaining to the operation of the boat and keep a finger on the pulse of things.

Sunday, second day out was a slow, lazy time. Passengers had an opportunity to walk uptown in Louisville to an early mass, get a newspaper or just look around. Soon after ten o'clock departure time the dining room was the setting of a half-hour non-denominational religious worship service conducted by the hostess. All were welcome to attend. It was a peaceful hour when all could meditate and enjoy the river scenery through the windows on either side of the cool dining room on the lower deck.

There was no more appropriate setting for the singing of hymns, particularly "Shall We Gather at the River," which was requested regularly. Usually this quaint service was well attended, though there were many who preferred a Sunday paper out on deck or would catch up on their rest after a difficult first night if they had felt out of their

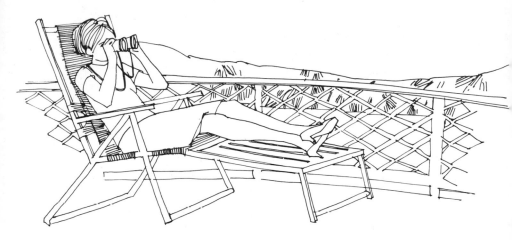

familiar surroundings of home and their own bed. Soon lunch was served, and the afternoons were restful now that the passengers had begun to settle down and get acquainted with their table partners or next room neighbors. Blood pressures were all lower as food, rest and pleasant surroundings do wonders for the human being.

Monday morning we landed at Evansville, Indiana for a shore stop. Later on, down past Cave-In-Rock by the late afternoon, our passengers were alerted to the wonders of a real pirate's cave on the Ohio. If navigation conditions permitted, they were given an opportunity to visit it. And the big brown and white dog which met us there regularly always welcomed a handout of a few steak bones from our cook house. There was a narrow path around the river's edge which gave all a chance to take a peek into the mysterious cave of Ohio River fame.

Maids and porters and other off-watch crew members joined the passengers in getting a little exercise on this surprise stop which was unusual and always added to the good feeling of everyone.

Particularly if one is a stranger to the Tennessee River and its meandering way of life, a trip to Kentucky Lake through Kentucky Dam is a fascinating experience. Twenty-two miles downstream from this dam at the confluence of the Tennessee and Ohio Rivers rests the unique little town of Paducah, Kentucky. With approximately two hundred passengers on a round trip from Cincinnati to Kentucky Lake, the *Delta Queen* always made a service stop here around midnight Monday, or, depending on navigation conditions such as fog or delays at the locks, a few hours later. At Paducah, soiled linens were entrusted to a six-hour laundry service, drinking water tanks were replenished and mail dispatched. The boat was usually quiet until around daybreak when a few early risers would stroll around the dew-covered decks peering up at the levee for whatever it might present while they awaited the beauty of sunrise on the river.

At six o'clock, three loud booms of the big silver bell on the top deck would summon everything to life. Deck hands began to untie and haul away at four-inch lines which had been secured in the ring bolts on the levee. Bells from the engine room announced that full steam was up, rudders shifted into position, the Captain from the bridge shouted, "Let her go", and the *Delta Queen* backed out into the river, the big paddle wheel splashing toward the dam.

All along the river, creatures were waking: white and gray heron would gracefully wing their course along the misty shore from willow to willow while occasionally a catfish leaped completely out of the water, breaking the glassy

reflection in the river's smooth surface. On either side near
the shore were dozens of small skiffs dragging the water for
mussels, whose shells were later processed and shipped to
button factories.

Suddenly a long blast on the whistle announced that
Kentucky Dam was approaching, and all decks were soon
alive with curious and eager passengers. They had hurried
through their second cup of coffee at breakfast and were assembling at various points on deck with their cameras and
binoculars, to get the best view of this mysterious locking
process.

A gigantic concrete lock chamber loomed at close
range and it seemed as if the boat would crash head on
into the wall. However, with guiding orders from the experienced captain to deck hands and pilot, the steamer would
glide safely into the lock chamber. There would be only a
few harmless bumps back and forth against the wall, and
after several unsuccessful attempts, the steel pin in the
floating steel post in the lock wall would be lassoed by the
deck hands and they would wind the opposite end of the
rope tightly around a capstan on main deck. One blast of
the whistle would echo back and forth through the dark
concrete cavern, telling the lock master that the boat was
all fast and ready to be lifted to the upper level. The mas-
sive iron valves would then be opened, water would gush
into the lock chamber, and the *Delta Queen* would be
slowly lifted fifty-six or more feet.

As the boat reached the upper level, daylight would
begin to appear and bright morning sunshine broke over
the lake. Approximately a mile and a half wide and one
hundred and eighty-four miles long, it was all formed by
Kentucky Dam.

The *Delta Queen* would cruise lazily throughout the
day on this man-made lake, perhaps tieing up at one of the

inviting state parks located along its shores, where swimming, horseback riding and fishing were available to any and all.

Prized color slides and pictures of this steamboat trip on the *Delta Queen* to Kentucky Lake by way of Kentucky Dam, the first step of the famed Tennessee Valley Authority water stairway to the south, would be shown by our river travellers when they returned home. On the return trip to Cincinnati the passengers were on a first name basis and it was easy sailing for the social department. Friday night everyone would be a little sad to say goodbye to all the new friends, and many kept in touch with those they had met on the trip. Many couples met on the river, romance entered their lives, and we would one day receive an announcement of the wedding. And it all started when they met on the *Delta Queen.*

While these delightful week trips were great for the guests, the crew's duties meant starting out every Saturday night with a new crowd and going through the whole selling process again for ten weeks in a row. We thought we had a new disease to report to the medical profession: brought on by tight summer schedule, minimum of time ashore, hot weather and general boat problems, it was called *Delta Queen*-itis. The symptoms were most likely to manifest themselves about the middle of August. Tempers would become a little short, some would threaten to, or actually would quit their job. The crew indeed lost much of the thrill of the sight of a new busload of tour groups heading over the hill for the boat.

Sometimes there would be a mixup in reservations and some unsuspecting lady would discover she was assigned by her agent in Brooklyn to an upper berth in a non-air-conditioned room, when she had requested a twin bed in Group A Parlor. It was a challenge to us all to iron

out some of these errors and keep everyone happy no matter what. These were the conditions which brought on the
strange malady known only to *Delta Queen* crew members.

On one of the very first Kentucky Lake trips we decided to share this one day with everyone who cared to get out
of bed early enough to catch the boat at Paducah and pay
five dollars fare. Aside from allowing more people to enjoy
a ride to the dam and the lake it would acquaint them
with our boat and bring in some badly needed extra revenue. And so advertising was carried in the Paducah papers
to see what the idea would produce.

Anyone could just come on board with the proper fare,
no advance reservations were required for the day and
lunch was included. We were flabbergasted at the onslaught streaming down over the levee. The purser was on
duty at his window in the office as on any other trip. They
came like a line of ants headed for a hole in the sugar barrel, men, women, children in arms, toddlers in hand.
Everyone was in a hurry, climbing up the stairs fluttering
five dollar bills in the air to pay and scramble for a deck
chair. The poor purser was overwhelmed. Some paid in
one dollar bills. Money was thrust in the window reckless-
ly, some fell on the floor and some piled in the cash box in
a disorderly heap. It seemed as if the entire population of
southwest Kentucky had answered the small newspaper ad.

Amid this melee was one lone passenger, Mr. Flam,
who had booked passage from Paducah to Cincinnati one
way. A misunderstanding on his part as to what time the
boat reached Paducah, combined with a slight fog delay
meant that this man had stood, sat or leaned on the levee
at Paducah since midnight. And he was not happy about it.
He was uninhibited in conveying to the purser his feelings
on the matter. The purser, in a desperate effort to please
Mr. Flam immediately called the porter, who escorted him

to his comfortable air-conditioned room where, evidently exhausted from his experiences of the night, he fell prone across the bed, fully dressed, and soon was snoring away. As soon as the boat pulled away from shore with these special Paducah passengers plus our regular round-trippers, the purser summoned the hostess.

"Esther," he said in quiet tones, "please give Mr. Flam a good table reservation. He's mad as hell, for he waited here on the levee all night for this boat. He's in his room now but I think you had better call him to the office at his convenience and do all you can to keep him happy."

"Sure, sure, Charley, I'll do all I can. Let's see, Mary Greene and her friend Carol Grimm have a table to themselves. I'll just put him there. Eating with the Captain's daughter ought to please him and he'll feel extra special."

With this, Ester went to the microphone, "Calling Mr. Flam: Will you please drop by the office at your convenience for your table reservation, Mr. Flam. . ." She repeated the message.

Soon a nondescript swain appeared at the office and said meekly, "Did you call me? Did I hear my name over the P.A. system?" He couldn't believe it. Esther was amazed to see such a mild-tempered young man, quite different from what she had imagined from the purser's report.

"Yes, Mr. Flam, you are to take table twelve. You will have as your table partners the Captain's daughter and her friend Miss Grimm. We are sorry that you were discommoded, but I'm sure you'll be pleased with your seating arrangement and we'll do all in our power to see that you're well cared for."

The young man thanked Esther profusely, confused and puzzled as to why he was selected from this mob of Paducah passengers to have lunch with the Captain's daughter.

His horoscope had predicted, however, that he'd have some unusual romance that day. So he smiled, pocketed his meal ticket nervously, and walked with a spring in his step in anticipation of the lunch hour. In the meantime, the real Mr. Flam, who had been sound asleep, awoke famished, and with renewed anger. He hadn't yet gotten a table reservation or any food. Leaping from his room, he fast made his furious way to the office. This time his anger approached the explosion mark as he assailed the purser, nearly threatening him with bodily injury if he wasn't assigned a table reservation at once and something to eat.

Charley paged Esther, the hostess, upset at her lack of attention to his orders earlier in the morning. Esther took one look at the Mr. Flam at the office window and made a mental note of his huge figure and prominent Roman nose as opposed to the little fellow she'd assigned to table twelve with the Captain's daughter.

Oh, for the floor to swallow her up before this fire-breathing dragon did. She'd assigned table twelve to a Mr. Flim, one of the novel Paducah day travelers instead of Mr. Flam from New York. The error was corrected, her life was spared, but Esther never lived down her reputation of flim-flaming Mr. Flam.

Somehow we got through that day. And we were indeed relieved to deliver the short-term passengers back to Paducah. Later, however, on similar trips we were well prepared with proper change at a special table on main deck and everything but special safety guards. All went well and after two or three of these trips everyone within miles had had a day on the lake and we discontinued this one day service.

When the summer was finally over and even the heavy Labor Day trips had passed, it was a relief to have five quiet days off for a breather before starting on the St. Paul trip. Later, the season would be finished off with New Orleans cruises. All these were lazier, less hurried and very pleasant.

After the first few days of a cruise, people became better acquainted, and if there was any suggestion of a standoffish atmosphere among the passengers, a stop at Paducah would change that. After a couple of hours at the Ervin S. Cobb Hotel or the Five-Twenty-Five Club, where mint juleps were a specialty and the Big Apple was another highly recommended drink, many who had been aloof or unapproachable came back to the boat with their arms around each other singing and greeting everyone they saw.

The hostess then knew she had nothing to worry about for the remainder of the cruise. Knowing they were in good hands and among friends, they all let down their barriers on to St. Paul and New Orleans. Paducah became a town long remembered for the many friends the *Queen* made.

7

NEW ORLEANS
FLOOD TRIP

In 1950 the *Delta Queen* left Cincinnati on the crest of a flood, headed for the Mardi Gras festivities in New Orleans. The wickets at the dams were all down, creating an "open river," and the boat, helped along by a swift current, was making fifteen miles per hour, which was pretty fast. As soon as we got past the bridge which crosses the Ohio near its confluence with the Mississippi at Cairo, Illinois, we would have nothing to impede our way, we thought. There were few bridges on the lower Mississippi.

In high water, a careful check was kept as to the number of feet and inches registered on the gauge at every bridge. Since we knew the height of the *Delta Queen* from the water level to the top of the pilot house, a fairly accurate estimate could be made, in advance, of our chances of safe clearance. We had cleared the Henderson, Kentucky bridge with no problem, and now only the Cairo bridge remained. But the river was rising below Evansville.

This was an important trip, and we were doggedly determined to clear at Cairo even if the roof of the pilot house had to be removed, drastic as that might seem. As is customary in high water, we had the smoke stack properly bent back by means of a huge hinge, cutting the stack's height by half. The pilot house and "cook house" stove pipe extended higher than the main smoke stack, but our calculations indicated a safe clearance by a margin of a few inches. However, on a rising river that figure was momentarily diminishing.

The black February night air was chilly, and filled with a fine, misty, rainy fog making visibility poor. The shore lights reflected that peculiar slick look which prevails when the river is swollen and out of her banks. Willow and other branches drooped to dabble in the muddy waters, heavy driftwood followed the swift current amidstream, and occasionally a treacherous log banged heavily against the side of the boat's steel hull, or tangled noisily and clumsily in the wooden paddle wheel. Trips such as this were murder on bucket planks and gave the carpenter a laborious job of repairing the wheel upon her return to home port.

Electric lights inside the cabin were dimmed to keep the reflections from blinding the pilot. News was soon bandied about among the crew, "The lights from the Cairo bridge are coming in sight". All attention for that moment focused on top deck near the paddle wheel and her accompanying misty spray, to watch the *Queen* go under the bridge. Everything possible had been done to load her heavily in the water, oil tanks and water tanks had been freshly filled, to make ready for the fast approaching bridge.

So that the boat could be better controlled, it seemed advisable to turn around far above the bridge and back downstream, underneath. This way the boat would work against the force of the swift current instead of being shoved by it. So that they could best view the action, most passengers were assembled on deck wearing their rain apparel. The *Queen* came ahead a few feet, stopped, floated backwards toward the bridge, stopped, came ahead a few turns, stopped and floated back in this see-saw fashion, carefully steered between the piers of the bridge.

The mate was stationed with a measuring device on a ladder near the top of the pilot house, where he could get a good visual angle of the amount of clearance as the *Queen* neared the crucial moment. The smoke from the bent stack boiled down over the top deck, and seemed to settle there too long in the heavy atmosphere.

For what seemed like an endless twenty minutes we see-sawed back and forth until: Here we go, right under the bridge! It looked as if we could surely reach up and touch the girders. Everyone held his breath—She'll go, no she won't, ooo-ooh! Through at last, until the bridge was in front of us as we looked back. The crash we heard was only the one joint of small stovepipe from the cook house, which crashed into the bridge and bent back like a giant straw. What a relief! The mate gave a loud hurrah as the boat cleared and everybody yelled and cheered from the decks.

The mate shouted, "I could get a dollar bill between the pilot house and the bridge but a five dollar bill would never have made it." As happy as we were, the passengers clapped long and loud. Captain Tom called out, "Everyone to the dining room now, we'll have music and dancing

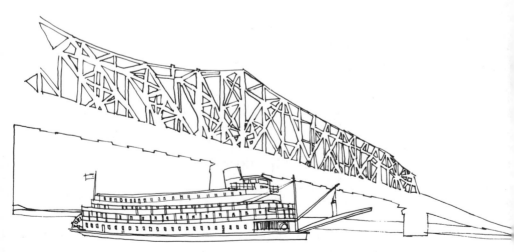

on down the Mississippi to New Orleans." Tom was requested at the piano unanimously and all joined in a spirited dance session to the music of "When the Saints Go Marching In."

Yet another hazardous point remained before we reached New Orleans. In concerned don't-alarm-anyone tones the question, "Do you know what time we'll reach the Greenville Bridge?" was asked at the breakfast table in the crew's dining room. That bridge was high enough for the *Delta Queen* to pass under, but in flood stage it was one we would be glad to have behind us. A strong current there in high water had been known to present problems. Only a few years before, a towboat plowing upsteam was caught by the force of the current; as she puffed and struggled mightily against it, she was swung around and her barges crashed against the bridge piers. This resulted in heavy loss.

It was about ten o'clock on a cool sunny Wednesday morning. I was inside the main cabin watching anxiously as we approached Greenville bridge, noting the strong wild current as it dashed twenty feet high against the concrete piers. As we drew nearer, suddenly I heard and felt a dull thud which seemed to shock the *Queen* clear through. I turned to the purser, who was nearby, and asked, "Bob, what was that?"

"This heavy current hitting the wheel, I think," he replied doubtfully. At that moment I realized the boat was out of control, turning around and floating sideways toward the bridge.

"Oh God, the tiller line's broken," I gasped. I ran up the stairs to get my seven-year-old, Jane, out of bed. I felt nauseated as I reached the top deck and started back toward Parlor J. Just as I reached her room, I could see the boat was fanning completely around, safely between the two piers. She was soon headed upstream below the bridge, where we anchored and tied up to a tree on shore. What a relief! I was still weak from fear.

The engineers and deck hands toiled all day amid the grease and muck, making tedious repairs to the steel cable tiller line which had broken. It was twisted and snarled as if demonstrating the devil's strength. When that part of machinery broke, the boat was helpless, like an automobile without a steering gear. I'm sure the engineers that day exhausted their repertoire of epithets for the *Queen* and her exasperating bad habits. I hasten to assure you that type of steering gear was soon replaced by a fool-proof hydraulic system. That ended the older tiller-line problem forever. It had been a number one necessity, along with new burners, on the boat's list.

"Ignorance is bliss" was proven that morning when Tom rushed down the stairway in the middle of this emergency on his way to the main deck. A dear old gentleman stopped him to proffer his complaint that his coffee at breakfast was not hot enough to suit him. He was completely unaware of the boat's serious and immediate difficulty. A lady relaxing in a deck chair nearby remarked, "What do you know, we're going under a bridge sidewise. It was exciting to pass underneath the Cairo bridge backwards but nothing like variety, eh?"

The circulation pump got to kicking up its heels downriver a little later the same day and the chief engineer spent the remainder of the day diagnosing, prescribing and applying medication to its troubled parts, and getting its bad disposition improved. Someone at the crew's table that evening said, "I'll bet Frank Heath (the engineer) won't forget his fifty-first birthday, February 14, 1950."

While nonexistent today, these problems were very much a part of those first years when we were getting acquainted with Her Majesty the *Queen,* and learning how to manage her unpredictable disposition.

On down the Mississippi the levees were in plain sight. One could see over the top and get that rare view of the vast areas which they protected. One could see factories, rain-splashed villages, huge plantations, beautiful stately southern mansions as they stood proud and defiant of old man river and his threatening tantrums. All these are the rare sights reserved for flood stage, when the boat rides high and majestically as if to review her domain of the Mighty Mississippi.

At floodtime or not, a steamboat trip on the Mississippi to New Orleans is just as romantic as it sounds. Entering the harbor which shelters miles of ships from every port of the world, many exchanging salutes with the *Delta Queen* as she proudly plied through the deep waters to her assigned berth alongside the great expanse of dock space, was a thrill to us all. There were ships loading and unloading sacks of coffee, bananas and many products from all foreign countries. There were battleships, passenger ships, oil tankers and freighters from foreign waters.

New Orleans meant the French Quarter, the Cabildo, Bourbon Street, horse-drawn buggies offering rides through the quarter, Dixieland music and jam sessions at the Parisian room. And Preservation Hall, wonderful French restaurants, charming patios, perfume and doll shops, pet alligator shops, Pirates' Alley lined with artists displaying their fascinating works, and the market place.

We could take a trip to the bayous or a motor trip to Biloxi, or a harbor excursion on the steamboat *President;* we could eat oysters Rockefeller and pralines and see Spanish moss and live oak trees. All these vivid memories give me goose pimples. Those who have been to New Orleans by steamboat know in part what I mean. Those who haven't may never know, but to me it is all bound up as a part of the countless cruises made to New Orleans aboard the steamboat *Delta Queen.*

: 8 :   CAPTAIN TOM'S FANS

CAPTAIN TOM's personality could not be forgotten by any who ever knew him. He loved people and they loved him. He would invariably tell me in his letters home from a trip aboard the boat, "This is the finest crowd we've ever had." I expected the passengers to gradually become so perfect, that they would be too wonderful for this world. Tom had a natural knack at handling a crowd, and an informal homey, comfortable atmosphere prevailed wherever he went. He played drums, xylophone, banjo and piano, entirely by ear. Even though he didn't read music, whenever he heard a melody whistled, he could improvise in an incredible fashion. When he walked into the entertainment area with an unlit cigar in his mouth and said, "Move over, son, let me have a turn at it," sat down at the piano and started in on "When the Saints Go Marching In," a crowd would be around him in no time watching that heavy left hand bass as his nimble fingers touched up and down the keys. The arthritics and octogenarians soon would join the younger ones in dance and those who couldn't get up tapped their feet. He had a magnetism and natural music talent like no one else I ever knew.

A post symphony party was held in the home of a friend in Hyde Park in Cincinnati at the time Thor Johnson was conductor. The program that night was the world premiere of our Louisville friend Claude Almond's *Steamboat Symphony,* and we were his guests. During the eve-

ning one of the Louisville guests approached Tom and said, "Tom, get in there and give us some music, river style." In the presence of all the dignified professional musicians and music lovers Tom hesitated to come on strong with his kind of music. "Aw, C. W., get Thor Johnson out of there and I will. I don't think he'd appreciate my stuff," Tom smiled as he answered.

"Say, Thor Johnson would give his right hand to be able to do what you can with your left," C. W. Stoll joked. Tom played, and all formality was shattered at once. He was like that.

Tom and his brother Captain Chris were a good team. Chris, the elder, was usually the more practical one and his opinion was highly respected by Tom. When any important question arose, Tom would always turn to General Manager Chris for a final decision, knowing him to be more conservative and of sound judgment. An aunt was once commenting on how well they worked together in the boat business. She said, "Now Tom, you're the wheel and Chris is the rudder. You're the pusher and he steers things right."

Chris replied "Yeah, Aunt Flo, and you know what people do to the rudders." (They were located in a direct line from the rest rooms.) Chris' humor was good natured but dry.

It was aboard the old *Gordon Greene* that a very elegantly dressed young lady from New York appeared one sailing day. She might have been labeled Mrs. Bergdorf Goodman Saks Fifth Avenue herself, with furs dragging in the dirt. The boat was quite different, I'm sure, from anything she'd ever experienced, with women sitting around exchanging cake recipes and crochet patterns as they rocked back and forth on the pleasant decks of the *Delta Queen's* predecessor. This lady, the epitome of style and sophistication, turned to her traveling companion and in a deep husky voice exclaimed, as she threw her sable furs over her arm, "This place is just too damned folksy for me." She, however, tipped her porter generously and soon got settled in her cramped stateroom. Before the trip had gone far, she was right in the groove of Mississippi River steamboating, had let down her Park Avenue barriers, and was doing the Paw Paw Patch, Hokey Pokey and Virginia Reel with everyone else. The spirit had been irresistible.

One man came to the *Delta Queen* with a ticket which had been sold to him by his travel agent back home who had not, however, given him exact knowledge of what he was to experience. The customer's only prerequisite had been that it be a restful vacation, away from home, family, friends and business. He was half sick and very tired. Before the week was over his health was restored, his mind refreshed and nerves calmed. When he left the boat, he gave us a tearful farewell, promising that this would be a repeat performance for him every year. It was for many years. We never forgot Burton, and how much this week on the river meant to him.

Stiff dignified professional men or business executives would declare their friends back home would never believe it if they could see them on the boat, partaking in the mock wedding, all made up perhaps as the pretty, pregnant bride, or as her father with a shotgun at the groom's back as they marched up the aisle all dressed up in improvised costumes of old curtains, and out of style evening clothes procured from my closet or a rummage sale.

Then there was the little friend from St. Louis whose doctor always prescribed a trip on the *Delta Queen* when she was recuperating from any affliction that overtook her. She never missed an early sunrise from the decks of the boat nor a bingo game. Her total number of cruises was well over two hundred, for she also traveled with us when in perfect health.

A very high percentage of boat passengers left at the end of a cruise with a feeling of having enjoyed one of the finest and most unique vacations in their entire experience. At Christmas time, Tom received greetings from hundreds of persons, many of whose names he could not fit to a face but who had ridden the boats, knew him and well remembered his wonderful hospitality. His friends were legion.

: 9 :   TRAGEDY

AT THE TIME of my husband's sudden death July 10, 1950,
I was too grief stricken and dazed to realize fully the impact this tragic loss would have on me or my family's future life, not to mention the effect on the fate of the *Delta
Queen*. I was alone in St. Mary's Hospital in Evansville,
Indiana near the end of the day. Only that morning I had
come along in the ambulance from the boat, where we had
docked at the public levee for a shore stop en route to Kentucky Lake. Every effort known to heart specialists was
tried in a vain attempt to save Tom's life.

My numbed mind could hardly handle the sad but
immediate task of calling all the various persons in other
cities to try to get things in order for funeral arrangements,
and the pangs that confronted me. Mary, our oldest, was in
Interlocken Music Camp in Michigan; our three younger
children were aboard the *Delta Queen* on their way to
Kentucky Lake under the watchful care of Carolyn Dority,
a young girl who had been near to our family and was now
working aboard the *Queen*. Our close friend, Margaret
Cramer of Cincinnati was a native of Evansville. She kindly called two of her friends there and told them of my circumstances. They came to the hospital and took me in tow
for the night at the McCurdy Hotel. I shall forever be
grateful to those two ladies who stuck by me so lovingly
and kindly, neither of whom I'd ever seen before.

An age-long sleepless night somehow passed. At the

break of dawn, we sat outside on the cool porch of the hotel, with its beautiful formal gardens in front, overlooking the river. It was a view forever impressed on my mind, as I awaited my limousine for the airport and a flight home to Cincinnati at nine a.m.

Mary, seventeen, was on her way home from Michigan, her very first flight, and the three younger children were safely placed on a midnight train at Paducah, Kentucky for the twelve-hour trip home. Gordon, fourteen, rose to the occasion to look after his seven-year-old sister Jane and twelve-year-old brother Tom en route. The next few days were like a waking dream—I couldn't believe what had happened, but somehow it all passed. I stood alone with four steamboats, four children, a broken heart and puzzled mind.

My friends and business associates tried to help. One solution after another was proposed, none of which ever proved to be perfect. Our very good advisor and friend Fred Cramer, a stockholder in Greene Line, took over as General Manager. He lived only two years. My kind sister who was so helpful to me in tight spots and to whom on most occasions I could turn to for help with my children, lived only a few months after Mr. Cramer's death.

Gordon, fourteen, secured a special permit to drive the car to help out at home. Mary was enrolled to go away to college in September. The *Delta Queen* was heavily mortgaged. I had very little business training, and almost more responsibility than I could handle in my fate-imposed position.

I can never forget my despair at the time as I puzzled over what to do, where to turn first, and seemed to find few answers. A sale for fifty cents on the dollar would have appealed to me. I was president of the company, and was to be plunged into more active management after Mr. Cra-

mer's death. I enrolled in the University of Cincinnati for
a night course in accounting. This seemed sensible. I also
undertook to learn typing, but night classes at Hughes
High School on top of those at the University proved to be
too much, and I never learned to type properly.

Even now, I get confused as I recall it all. Chapters of
my life I'd like to erase, but they are behind me now, like
a storm that tore through with tornado force, leaving behind a devastated area that called for adjustment to a new
life.

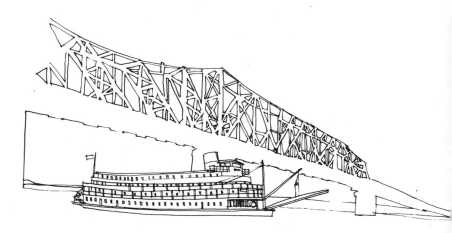

: 10 :   FILLING TOM'S SHOES

THE ADJUSTMENT period following Tom's death was difficult. One steamboat captain followed another in an attempt to replace him. Due to the seasonal aspect of steamboat work it has often been a difficult matter to secure
capable and suitable help. The *Delta Queen* had been pretty
much of a one-man-managed operation. My husband had
worn many caps. He was captain first of all, but a trip to
the pantry to check on a new coffee urn, or to check the
ability of the newly hired salad man made him steward, a
trip to the cook house to taste a new dish the chef was
trying out for the first time would make him cook. After a
fill in period at the piano when the regular man was taking
a breath of air, he became musician. Out on deck he
would act as the mate to settle an argument between deck
hands and in the pilot house when the pilot on watch took
a few minutes break, he became pilot.

Since his brother Captain Chris's death in 1944, Tom
had inherited the title General Manager. In addition to all
these duties he often made use of an unsold parlor aboard
the boat, where he would set up a typewriter on a card table and personally answer many important letters by
"hunt-and-peck system." So it was a big order for anyone
to fill Tom's place. It couldn't be done in reality, but we
all tried. Athough rearing my family was a full time job,
problems with the boat and a multitude of decisions to be
made could not be ignored.

The elements played a great part in our business. I still get a little itchy when rain falls two or three days in succession around the middle of January. If three zero nights appeared in succession, particularly if the river was at a normal or what is known as "pool stage" we could expect ice. The Mardi Gras trip to New Orleans, which fell about this time of the year, was always a source of much needed revenue at a time when the barrel was low following a long winter's lay-up. If it became necessary to cancel this trip due to navigational difficulties, we had to know it well enough in advance to notify our passengers, as many of them came from distant places. Weather reports were as important to us as stock market reports are to a financial tycoon.

In case flood waters began to creep up, rain continued and the forecast was not good, the wharfboat watchman began to pull in. This involved the use of an electrically controlled capstan on the wharfboat connected by mammoth linked chains secured to thick iron rings on the levee near the top of the hill. The wharfboat containing Greene Line offices, to which the *Delta Queen* was lashed, was gradually pulled up by these chains as the river rose, until the wharfboat could go no further. Then, as the water started leveling out over the top of the levee, wide boards were placed at the end of the wharfboat stage to allow cars or pedestrians to come aboard the wharf. If the flood waters really got out of hand a skiff was used to ferry the office employees out from the city street to where they could step on the dry gangplank.

We listened avidly to the report of the gauge at various bridges during floodwaters, to determine our chance of clearing a bridge. On one occasion the *Delta Queen* left Cincinnati on a rising river for New Orleans. The flood came and went while the boat was on her three week trip,

and all was nearly normal when she returned. Another
time the K & I bridge at Louisville, Kentucky looked to be
a problem. We were all anxiously awaiting news to see if
the boat would be able to clear the bridge on her return
trip from New Orleans. Two or three inches clearance

would make the difference. On this particular occasion the river was rising, and if the bridge was not cleared we would have to bring our passengers in by bus from Louisville to Cincinnati for them to make their plane or train reservations. This of course meant loss of revenue, added expense and inconvenience for our guests.

That night the phone rang. I recognized Captain Underwood's voice, "Hello, that you Mrs. Greene? Well, we're here at the oil pile, everything fine."

A welcome message. I knew that if they had reached the oil dock where the boat took on fuel then they had cleared the bridge, as the oil dock was a mile or more further upstream. They had cleared the bridge by a mere two inches.

Another time, the *Gordon Greene* had to anchor below this bridge and wait patiently for the water to recede. This played havoc with our schedule. The problem is not so pertinent today with the newly built, immovable dams on the Ohio, because if the stage of the water is too high for the boat to go under the bridge, neither can she go through a lock chamber. It seems simpler that way.

The *Delta Queen* presented the problems of a ship, a restaurant, a night club, a motel, and government rules and regulations done up in a neat wrapping of wind, fog and rain, tied with a fancy wide bow of fun, romance, pleasure and restful vacations for thousands of river travelers. As I look back from where I stand today it seems nothing short of a miracle that we kept the *Delta Queen* going through those adjustment years. But I think there are times when the Lord did provide, for we couldn't have done it alone.

: 11 :

THE BAR

CAPTAIN GORDON GREENE, the founder of Greene Line Steamers, would never permit a bar to be operated aboard any of the Greene Line boats. He did not drink alcoholic beverages, nor did he believe in drinking. He made his profits from the boats without the sale of liquor. This theory was carried out with every boat of the fleet up to the *Gordon Greene.*

By this time prohibition had come and gone and the public began to demand the services of a cocktail lounge. A question which usually accompanied any request for a reservation was, "Have you a bar aboard the boat?" On the *Gordon Green* beer was sold and set-ups for any drinks a passenger might want, but when the *Delta Queen* was acquired, operating a bar seemed inevitable. Captain Mary was in favor of carrying out the rigid policy of her husband in this respect, but times had changed and she was finally convinced that it would be all right to own a bar. It was pointed out to her that it was better to serve drinks in a controlled manner from a bar than have them consumed in a less dignified manner.

So we had a bar, with all the headaches of the business. Bartenders were not always too reliable, and there was much chance of loss in that phase of the business, from thievery, dishonesty, and other scheming tricks. It was a necessary evil. One year, it seemed wise to farm the liquor business out to someone whom we felt was reliable, and

take the profits on a percentage basis. He'd buy his own
stock, be his own mixologist and pay us "off the top." He
always liked to have an attractive barmaid to serve the passengers more efficiently in the dining room and in the evenings during the entertainment. At times it proved to be
an advantage.

The barmaids, however, came and went. Most of them
have faded from memory, except a few never to be forgotten.

One had coal black hair, had seen better years long
ago, but worked hard. She could well recommend her
wares, for she imbibed frequently. Her forthright manner
of speech was impressive, and she did not apparently have
too much real affection for her boss-man as he vainly tried
to inspire her to keep her hair well-dressed, and her appearance neat and attractive. One day at the crew's dining
table, when all had gone about their business, she sat for a
few minutes to rest and discuss the day's problems with a
musician.

"I tell you, I've been so damn busy today I ain't had
no time to change my clothes."

"The bar's been busy. This has been a drinkin' crowd,
all right."

"That man, he thinks I should look like Hedy Lamarr
or somebody all the time, and still he keeps yellin, 'get out
there and get some orders from the dining room. I need
some cold beers out of the refrigerator, be sure to wipe
them ash trays good, get a mop here, this corner is
leaking. . . .'" I just get fed up. Then he says, 'Marlene
your hair's stringing over your face, you need to use some
"Ban", and when did you do your nails last?' " He lit into
me this morning and I'd just had all I could take. I said,
"Mr. Baron, damn it, you get out there: trade jobs with
me, keep your head in a beer barrel all day and see what
your hair looks like."

"Oh, Marlene, I guess we all have our troubles, don't we?" Harmon answered.

A few days later the boat was beating her path up the Tennessee River, in a section noted for catfish and an occasional water moccasin. One revolution of the wheel picked up one of these snakes and threw it right onto the fantail from where it crawled up into the engine room and lay, as if stunned, in open view. Marlene had tipped the bottle a little more than usual that day. When she walked out of the bar toward the area of the engine room to get a breath of fresh air, she saw that snake on the deck, let out a piercing scream, ran back into the crew's dining room and loudly declared she'd never touch another drop. She thought it was the D.T.'s for sure.

Just before Mardi Gras in 1962, flood waters were rampant in the Ohio. It seemed meaningful that a small tow boat named the *Mary B.* on her way upstream past Cincinnati in flood waters should experience a strange accident. For us at Greene Line it seemed to be a message of disapproval. The *Mary B.*, cause unknown, plowed smack into the starboard rear bulkhead of the *Delta Queen*, ripping a gaping hole in the side of the cocktail lounge as if to say, "There, that'll fix you, I never wanted that place added to the boat in the beginning." Captain Wagner, Vice President Caldwell and all help that could be summoned, worked long hours to get that repair work done within a week before the boat left for Mardi Gras on the crest of a flood.

: 12 :   ROCK ISLAND

MY FAMILY and I had put in many days redecorating our home. All day long I had rearranged furniture, hung pictures, and attended to other last minute details, spurred on by an anxious desire to see the effect of the new décor. That night I was invited to a party at the home of the Metz family, friends who lived in the beautiful Wyoming section of greater Cincinnati. The guest of honor was a young man who had been a choice passenger on the boats for many years. He had, in spite of a drastic physical deformity, which gave him the usual handicaps of a hunchback, won his way into the hearts of all who ever knew him. He was witty, musical, and possessed a magnetism seldom encountered.

Any party at which he was in attendance promised to be an interesting and pleasurable affair. I couldn't think of declining this invitation but I had made a mistake by using so much of my energy that day, without reserving enough for the evening at the Metz home.

We were all enjoying the lovely view of the city from the patio, the moon was bright over the valley, and Charley was strumming his banjo ukelele with all joining in a song now and then. Everyone was in a relaxed mood, and the thought of the new look of my own house in Hyde Park was especially satisfying to my mind. Suddenly the phone rang, and I recognized the voice of Horace Lyle, Assistant Manager of Greene Line.

66

"I'm sorry to disturb the party, but I just had a phone call from Captain Brasher. The boat's in Rock Island, and she has 'run thro' herself'." I stood speechless. As a million things went through my mind I didn't know what to ask first.

"Well, tell me about it, where and when? Anyone hurt? What'll we do?—she's filled with passengers, you know." Run through herself! Can any layman feel the full impact of such a catastrophe? How can a person run through himself? How disastrous can it be? This term applies to steamboats when a piston, on its mad way to push steam into the cylinders, lets go, due to a failure of some controlling strap of machinery best known to engineers. Instead of returning the way it should, to start another thrust, it keeps going headlong into the cylinder and either sticks there in a lopsided fashion or rams all the way through the cylinder head and maybe through the bulkhead in a ruthless manner, regardless of who or what may be affected on the other side of the wall. In case the disastrous irregularity occurs when the piston rod is going the opposite direction the whole works is thrown out and into the river near the wheel. In either case the boat is crippled like a horse with a broken leg. This time the piston had stuck fast in the cylinder in an off-center position.

After babbling over the phone in a one minute confused, the next stunned, manner for a few minutes I hung up and announced my problem to my hosts. I'm sure that while they were sympathetic with my plight, they were secretly glad they rested securely in the fold of Proctor and Gamble's well-known soap industry instead of a steamboat type of livelihood where something could "run through itself."

I excused myself and started for home, dazed from weariness and befuddlement. What was a woman, whose responsibility it was to manage a steamboat business, to do when the boat runs through herself with 190 passengers on board. At least, she didn't run through any of them.

I awoke next morning with all the aftereffects of a sleepless night. I started phoning for my precious sister to come to my rescue. She would help with the home fires and care for the children, while I drove to Rock Island, where the crippled boat had limped into harbor the day before. Mr. Lyle and I took turns driving and arrived about ten o'clock that night. There the *Delta Queen* sat. She looked all right from a distance as we drove down to the levee, but she must have had an awful scar somewhere.

The passengers seemed happy enough, some were dancing to the music which was carrying on in true "the show must go on" fashion, and others were playing cards or relaxing on deck. The only irregular excitement was evidenced by the engineering department working tirelessly in an attempt to free the cylinder of its unwelcome intruder. We were glad the thing had stuck, rather than going all the way through the cylinder head and into the wall. How to entice it back out was the problem.

Every device known to our engineering department was employed to try to free it intact. Since another piston had to be made, the present one was important as a pattern to follow. At last, they gave up this idea and started with blowtorches to bring the errant hunk of iron out in molten pieces. As I write these words a twist of the melted piston of the *Delta Queen* serves very well as a rusty gnarled paper weight on my desk.

We needed a miracle, for if the boat failed to be on her return to Cincinnati by the following Saturday, one week off, the three-week New Orleans cruise would have to be canceled. I visualized us slowly going out of business, with the bank mortgage still unpaid.

To get our minds off the disaster, we occasionally went ashore to dinner, and visited a few of the night spots in Rock Island but it was always back to the boat, and the clanging engine room, sweating engineers, and deck hands working feverishly away.

Andy Lodder, an officer of our company, had an idea. He thought of the *Delta King*'s machinery stored at Fulton Shipyards back in California, all identical to the *Queen*'s. Maybe the proper replacement for this thing we were melting to pieces was stored there, in good condition and workable. A phone call was made and luck was with us. The heavy piece of machinery was loaded onto a Flying Tiger freight plane from Fulton Shipyards and arrived at Quad City airport the next morning.

I had taken a sleeping pill prescribed by the ship's physician, in an effort to get some rest that day, but when I learned of the delivery of this shipment, I disregarded the idea of any rest and wandered around with heavy eyes and a dazed mind, watching every move of the delivery of this precious object. Work progressed on schedule and miraculously every last bolt was finally secured and all was ready to leave Rock Island in safe time, Saturday. The New Orleans cruise would leave as scheduled. Saved again!

There were a few other bits of unusual excitement at Rock Island. One of the dozens of cars which were daily parked on the levee there let go one afternoon, when our passengers were lazily relaxing on the peaceful decks of the boat, in the autumn sun. It tore down the hill in a mad rush, splashed on into the river, and rammed with a bang into the very side of the boat's steel hull. This event wasn't on the hostess' entertainment agenda for that day.

On the morning of departure, when we were all thankful to get out and away, one new passenger registered for the return cruise to Cincinnati. Her family, who seemed anxious to get her settled on the boat, hastily left. She was all ours. Not long after her arrival, we heard fire engines coming nearer and nearer. Yes, right to the river's edge and onto the boat rushed the firemen, hose in hand. A thin plume of mysterious smoke from near the pilot house had been noticed by someone on shore, who sent in an alarm. We couldn't figure how a smoldering fire could have been started so quickly in the painter's bucket on top deck while he went to buy a pack of cigarettes from the concession stand.

Later, the new lady passenger was stopped by the mate as she attempted to disconnect a section of the ship's fire-hose. A short time later, unexplainable smoke was seen pouring from a wastebasket in the linen room. That did it. We notified our insurance company and kept a twenty-four-hour vigil over the strange, beautiful but perhaps demented girl. The help of crew members was enlisted, and she was never allowed out of sight of a responsible person all the way to Cincinnati. She was one guest we were not sorry to discharge.

All this excitement at Rock Island, of course, made headlines in the newspapers—the old *Queen* was out front again! Newspaper stories were captioned "The Charred Hulk of the *Delta Queen* Limped Past Paducah, On Her Return To Cincinnati—Void Of All Passengers."

The truth was, she had no damage other than an attack of "run-thru-itis", and her passengers all signed and presented to me an impressive document in appreciation of all that the crew of the *Delta Queen* had done toward their entertainment and welfare at Rock Island. This dilemma had been an adventure for them, and everyone was happy in spite of not having reached the scheduled destination on that first St. Paul trip. The passengers knew they could always make it next time and many of the same persons, God bless them, were aboard the next trip to the upper Mississippi.

When I arrived home after this anxious week, I was proud to find my new Venetian blinds installed and the house looking new and fresh. Still, after my routine physical check-up the following week, I was told my blood pressure was "up a little." I couldn't imagine why.

: 13 :   CHATTANOOGA TRIP

I HEARD slow footsteps in the gangway leading to my office, followed by a light tapping at my door. I looked up to see Captain Paul Underwood's face framed in the upper, glass section of the door. I motioned for him to come in.

"Mrs. Greene, got a minute?" he drawled in his Alabama accent.

"Sure Cap, have a seat. Be with you in just a minute." I was in the process of clearing my desk in preparation for leaving for the day. "What you got on your mind?"

"I've been thinkin', if you all give me the okay, I'll try bringin' the *Delta Queen* up through that old Wilson Lock when we're down at Muscle Shoals next trip. Then maybe you can schedule a cruise to Chattanooga next year. When they get the new Wilson Lock finished, of course there'll be no problem. But I know I can get the boat up through that old lock there now," he mused.

"There wouldn't be much room to spare, would there, Captain? Just what are the dimensions there?" I asked.

"Well, I'll tell ya', that lock chamber is just sixty feet wide. That'll leave two feet on the sides for the *Delta Queen's* fifty-eight feet, and with the lock chamber three hundred feet long, the *Delta Queen's* two hundred eighty-five feet would make it okay if we send the gangplank through ahead on a float, otherwise it would just stick out too far."

I envisioned a horribly risky job of navigation.

"Oh Captain, that would be pretty tricky, wouldn't it? Do you think it's safe and advisable?" I was doubtful.

"Oh sure it's safe. I can do it all right, if you all say so. The trips we used to make on the *Gordon Greene* to Chattanooga and Knoxville were mighty nice, you know."

"Yes, they were some of the best trips we ever made. But the little old *Gordon,* with only a fifty-foot beam, could go almost anywhere. I only wish the *Delta Queen* could go everywhere the *Gordon* went. Remember her trips up through those old hand-manipulated locks on the Cumberland River? And all those trips she made up the Kanawha River clear to the head of navigation! Up in my old stamping grounds to Montgomery, West Virginia. She'd nose right up under that bridge before turning around. And those mountains on either side! It looked like you could reach out and touch 'em. Then, of course Chattanooga. . . . They were all great trips," we reminisced.

"Yeah, I'll never forget how Harris and I always brought her up the Tennessee River around those bends near Chattanooga and how everybody raved over the scenery, Lookout Mountain and Signal Mountain in the distance, as we steered her up toward Moccasin Bend."

"Those are trips surely never to be forgotten. Tom always looked forward to them too. The Tennessee River trips were full of fun—remember the hush puppies, the catfish, the lemon meringue pie, at the Catfish Hotel, Pittsburg Landing, at Shiloh, Tennessee."

"My, my, yes, that was always a good stop and a good place to eat. Bet there's not another place like it in the world. Yeah, we'd be able to go to Chattanooga or at least to Hale's Bar. Of course, that's a little bottleneck now, but we could bus the passengers on in to Chattanooga. It's only fifteen miles or so! Or we could send them up on a smaller boat," the Captain debated persistently.

"It would be nice to go to Chattanooga," I agreed. Yet I wasn't too open-minded about the old Wilson Lock navigation problem. The thought of it sank to the pit of my stomach.

"Well, I know I can do it. It'll take careful navigation and little extra time, but if you give me permission I'll prove it can be done," the Captain smiled confidently. He got up from his chair and started toward the door.

"Give us a few days. We'll think it over. Let you know, Captain," I replied, as I opened my pocket book and started a search for my car keys.

The captain added, "You know, Mrs. Greene, that's my part of the country down there—Florence, Alabama. I know that river like the back of my hand. If I had doubts about it I wouldn't suggest such an idea, but you think it over and let me know," he said as he walked out the door.

On my way up Columbia Parkway toward my home in Hyde Park, I was thinking only of past trips to Tennessee River. There was the first trip when we traveled on the swift swirling current, long before the Kentucky Dam was ever started. My children had been alerted to look for turtles and snakes in Colbert Canal as we navigated through it around Muscle Shoals. Once the children found a dead water mocassin, held a funeral and buried it in the sand at the river's edge while the passengers all went through the National Cemetery at Shiloh Battlefield, Pittsburg Landing, Tennessee.

I can never forget our amazement once, when we saw a small lion tied up in someone's backyard in Decatur, Alabama as we took a walk around town during a shore stop. Another time, when we were entertained at dinner by the Chamber of Commerce in Chattanooga, at Lookout Mountain Hotel, a funny mix-up resulted in Greene Line receiving the bill for the occasion! This was corrected, of course, with the apologies of our hosts. And then there was the fascination of our first trip through Rock City and Ruby Falls. During the Second World War, how the ladies all scrambled for a precious pair of nylon hose available in Chattanooga, when we were lucky to have an old darned-at-the-heel pair of thick wrinkly rayon ones!

We made the trip again once, immediately following a session of measles in our family when Gordon had been so sick. One day he had said, "Aunt Vina don't go to school today, for I think I'm going to die." I risked the trip providing the children got into bed early and didn't go swimming. Then there was the time we all did go swimming in the river at Pittsburg Landing. Tom jumped for a high dive off the top deck into the deep water. This splashed Mrs. Harvey's World War II material skirt, shrinking it almost to her waist. I chuckled over the time Stella Kurtz and a group of friends were on their way back to the boat from a shore stop at one of the small Tennessee River towns. They had purchased a rare bottle of "bitters", and in order to conceal the forbidden purchase she had agreed to hide it inside her snuggies, which didn't prove to be too secure. Just as they approached the boat, the bottle slid, down, down, and amid screams, crashed to the ground. It shattered to bits, leaving a puddle of rare Tennessee Mountain Moonshine to drench the cobblestones.

Then, while Kentucky Dam was in the process of construction, the *Gordon Greene* landed one Sunday afternoon. Tom had the deck hands bring on board and saw up the logs saved from the burning heaps along the shore for our own living room fireplace in Cincinnati—enough for two years.

Oh yes, a trip to Chattanooga would be nice. I

stopped at a red light, made a right turn, parked, and went inside a Hyde Park supermarket to get a loaf of bread and a few groceries to fill out the menu for dinner. That night I dreamed of the Battle of Lookout Mountain. Captain Underwood was the General-in-Command. He was herding all the Confederate soldiers, who turned out to be *Delta Queen* passengers, up through the old lock at Wilson Dam with orders to "swim or die." I was awakened by the phone ringing in my ears.

"Say, did Captain Underwood mention anything to you about taking the boat up through Wilson Lock this trip, to Muscle Shoals?" It was Horace Lyle on the line.

"Yes, he did. Just as I left the office yesterday. Is he in there today?" I queried, looking at my watch, "I was awake long into the night thinking about Wilson Dam and Chattanooga, and I've overslept."

"Yes, he's here in the office now. Will you be in soon?" Lyle asked.

"Be down there as soon as I can make it. We can talk it over. Keep him around there, and is Andy Lodder in today? Get hold of him, and let's have a confab over this idea." I hung up, hurried through a fast breakfast, left the beds unmade, and took off.

The pros and cons of Captain Underwood's project were discussed with the "Ayes" having it. He'd try his luck at Wilson Lock next trip.

The passengers aboard the *Delta Queen* for the upcoming Muscle Shoals trip had a bonus thrill they didn't expect when Captain Underwood headed up toward old Wilson Lock. Everyone was on deck to watch her go through. Crew members who could leave their post of duty, as well as passengers, lined the railing to watch the procedure. At the dinner table the second mate remarked, "Captain, you're going to have to use a shoe horn to get the boat through that lock. Glad you're the pilot and not me."

Somehow, I had great confidence in Captain Underwood's ability to do this job without so much as a hard bump against the wall. Later, one of the waiters was overheard telling the pantry man "I'm telling you I was up on that top deck signifyin' to God every minute we were going through that lock!"

The fifty-eight by two hundred eighty-five-foot *Delta Queen* was safely steered into the sixty-by-three-hundred-foot lock, with the stage removed and sent ahead as planned. In a series of three steps the boat was lifted one hundred feet to the top level of water. It was as if the *Delta Queen* had been carried by crane and set down atop a downtown building—frightening, thrilling but safe. We were convinced. Now a regular cruise to Chattanooga would be on the 1957 schedule.

June of the next year, Chattanooga trip was a sellout. Many who had remembered the good old days of the *Gordon Greene* were pleased that this trip could once more be enjoyed on the more comfortable *Delta Queen*. We contacted a certain agency in Chattanooga and made an agreement with them to handle the bus tours for the one day we would be in Chattanooga. We had confidence in their ability to plan the schedule, provide guides, and transportation. They were instructed to pick up our passengers at Hale's Bar Dam fifteen miles down river from Chattanooga and offer the sights of the city, returning them at the end of the day. Greene Line was to deliver a boxed picnic lunch at a designated, recommended spot called the "Commons." The steward would bring the food and drink by means of a rented truck to the lunch spot by noontime.

However, lightning struck the lift bridge under which the *Delta Queen* had to pass near Bridgeport, Alabama some thirty-five miles below Chattanooga. It was damaged, and the repairs of the bridge were scheduled to begin the day the boat was in that area, and would stop navigation for a time. The authorities however, agreed to permit us to go up under the bridge, discharge our passengers at Hale's Bar and then come back down under the bridge before their work began. This meant our people would then be returned to Bridgeport, Alabama instead of Hale's Bar to board the boat after their day's sightseeing. This seemed to be the best arrangement possible and the only time lightning ever altered the *Delta Queen's* schedule.

Early in the morning the *Delta Queen* nudged into a dry mud bank at Hale's Bar and "choked" a tree along the shore. Passengers arose earlier than usual, foregoing their second cup of coffee at breakfast to scurry around with cameras and binoculars, getting all set for the day's sightseeing in Chattanooga. The weather forecast was fair and warm, but the cool early morning air was refreshing, and everything looked fine.

My daughter Mary was hostess aboard the boat at that time. She decided to join the bus tour and enjoy the sights of the city along with the passengers. Just as she was leaving the boat, she was surprised to be summoned to the purser's office.

"Mary," Bob the purser explained, "since you're going along, will you attend to the crowd in general—just see that there's no difficulty at the various places where there's an admission fee. Here's the correspondence file. Take it along to refer to if any problem arises. I'm sure everything will be O.K."

"Certainly Bob," Mary replied, "I'll be glad to," with no thought other than having an enjoyable day.

After seeing that all the passengers were comfortably seated, Mary climbed aboard the bus and found a seat not far from the driver, in case it should be necessary to communicate with him en route.

As the bus rolled along toward Chattanooga, the river's cool breeze wafted in through the windows, the trees in the hills took on a fresher green look after the night's fog, and an atmosphere of anticipation was evident among the passengers. Everything went fine until lunch time approached.

The bus driver turned out to be new on the job and didn't know where the "Commons" was located. He was confused as to just where to stop for lunch. Quiet low-toned conferences took place between Mary and the driver. The bus load of people was unaware that Mary was leafing through the correspondence in a frantic search for some clue as to where the "Commons" was located. The duty so recently imposed upon her suddenly took on the ominous terms of "Tour Conductor" for two bus loads of elderly people, with a driver new on his job and unacquainted with the city of Chattanooga.

They searched for a lunch spot unknown to anyone aboard the bus, as the Tennessee midday sun beat down hotter and hotter by the moment. By now everyone was hungry and looking forward to the box lunch which had been promised them at the "Commons" picnic grounds, a cool shady spot where food and rest would be available.

By some uncanny bit of luck the bus at last pulled to a halt at a sort of ballfield-playground where Mary announced, "All right everyone, out for the 'Commons.' Just make yourself comfortable—the food and cold drinks will be here soon." It had not been explained in the correspondence, however, just how older affluent people could be made comfortable at a ballfield in 90° weather without adequate shade amid grasshoppers, chiggers and ants.

One cantankerous old man refused to leave the bus.

The others scattered here and there trying to find a place to sit in the sparse shade or search for restrooms. Mary rued the minute she took over this duty, as she was always automatically upset if things were not just right for the passengers.

Jack Cleary, the steward, who had spent hours oversee-ing the delectably prepared box lunches was at this time struggling with a broken-down bus half way up Lookout Mountain. An hour later the truck jostled in miraculously. Jack, too, had located the "Commons." With sweat rolling down his face, his clean white shirt of the morning smeared with mud and grease, and swearing under his breath, he be-gan to distribute the food and cold drinks to relieve the fam-ished crowd. Oh! to get a hold of that so-called "agency" and the man who rented him this broken down truck.

By now every passenger had found a spot to sit down amid bugs and ants for rest, relaxation and food. The ship's elderly physician, Dr. Roller, his face aflame, and his white hair waving like one of the prophets of old attempt-ed to settle Mary's nerves with professional admonishments to keep calm and cool.

Lunch boxes were quickly opened; the fried chicken tasted good. One lady by mistake was handed a large box containing nothing but pickles. And, as she later ex-plained, she hated pickles. The mistake was corrected and after lunch, on to bigger and better things. There was Rock City with the Swinging Bridge, Fat Man's Squeeze, and other strange tourist attractions. Once one started through the narrow walkway, the best way out was to forge ahead. The temperature, past ninety in the shade by now, was a bit strenuous for a group of oldsters; just too much for one day. A little old man with a foreign accent ap-proached our organist with, "Oh, Harmon, I yust don't tink I can make it."

Harmon replied, "Just stick by me and we'll be all right. It's better to go on ahead rather than face this line and go back."

Next came the bus ride on to Ruby Falls which were located inside a deep cave. "At least it will be cool," thought Mary. The ride into the cave was a relief from the heat, but restrooms were in demand. Upon alighting from the bus one older lady came rushing out of the door marked "Ladies" as fast as she'd gone in with, "Oh, Mary there is no papah." By now what difference did it make. A provision for toilet tissue was not a part of the agency's agreement, and the situation was one which Mary was not equipped to take care of.

After the cave, the bus was a welcome sight to the by now foot-sore passengers, who felt they'd had a good look at Chattanooga highlights. Everyone gladly settled down for the thirty-five-mile ride back toward Bridgeport, Alabama and the *Delta Queen* with its comforts of home.

The old man who had refused to leave the bus proved to have a good reason. There he sat in the same position he had been in at first, puddles underneath his seat, trousers soaking wet, looking straight ahead with nothing to say. After all, how could one verbalize such a predicament.

Heads nodded, and the bus was quiet on the long ride back down the river. As the bus left the main highway and took off through the rough cornfield road in toward the river bank and the boat, the driver turned to Mary and casually remarked, "Have ya ever been on one of these things when they've turned ovah? They sure make a sickenin' sound."

We went to Chattanooga again in 1958 and subsequently for many years. However, never again did we follow any agency's plans. I, as president and general manager of Greene Line, personally made every arrangement for all activities offered in Chattanooga. After the first experience, we stayed there two days instead of one, gave our passengers a beautifully served hot lunch at one of the choice private clubs of Lookout Mountain and had the best of service everywhere. It was one of the most charming cruises of the *Delta Queen*.

Soon the new Wilson Lock was completed, making navigation easier, and by now the Hale's Bar bottleneck dam has been replaced. So a cruise all the way to Chattanooga is delightful and in great demand. The scenery is unsurpassed anywhere and offers an educational exposure to the T. V. A. area of the Tennessee River. It is one of my favorite cruises.

: 14 :   BIG ATTRACTION

THE *Delta Queen* was forever a source of widespread curious attraction at every port of call. In some of the larger
cities we were greeted by the mayor, news media, president
of the Chamber of Commerce, and other dignitaries, offering the key of the city to the Captain or company officials.
Special welcoming committees would assemble on board
the boat to direct the passengers to the popular shopping
areas and in some cases the courtesy of transportation to
town was furnished. Many passengers took the scheduled
tour offered by the boat, while others struck out on their
own to visit certain particular points of interest, or take a
long walk ashore.

The smaller towns often gave us a rousing welcome
with a peppy school band, lively music and gaily uni-
formed high-stepping majorettes. At any rate, wherever
we stopped we could depend on hundreds of sightseers eager to clamber aboard. Where possible we allowed them to
pay a visit, a limited number at a time.

The small towns of the south were particularly in-
triguing. The red clay banks of Alabama, with sweet fragrance of honeysuckle in the air, colorful mimosa trees in
fringed bloom, crepe myrtle at a deep red peak, mule
drawn wagons, vine covered porches, barking dogs, friendly southern accents—all filled the towns and villages with
personality and charm. This was a revelation to many of
our passengers who came from the rushed cities of the east,
and other faraway places.

On one occasion, one of our regular passengers, who had traveled numerous times on the *Delta Queen* decided to stay on the boat while the boat was docked in town to write letters, read, or just watch the people who came aboard as sightseers. She'd been to Chattanooga before, had taken the bus trip already and she loved just being on the boat. Miss Hall was a member of an aristocratic family of her home town, highly educated, and a cultured, lovable lady of means.

At the end of the day she and I sat on deck, chatting a few minutes after dinner. I said, "Miss Hall, you didn't go uptown, or on the tour. I hope you had a restful time and didn't mind staying on the boat all day."

She clasped my hand in both of hers and exclaimed "Oh, Mrs. Greene, I had a perfectly delightful time, just having the boat all to myself and watching the fascinating varieties of people who came on board. It was more entertaining than if there had been a special party planned in my honor."

"Yes, we do often see some unique people come down to look us over," I agreed.

"Mrs. Greene, I must tell you about one lady. She appeared to be past seventy, wore a stiffly starched gingham housedress, with an old fashioned bonnet to match. I hadn't seen such an outfit since I was a child. We engaged in conversation and I asked her where she lived. She answered, 'On a farm outer town aways.' She went on to say 'Lady, you're a citified woman, I kin tell by yer talk, and all them fine clothes.' Really, I was wearing a very simple dress with this sweater over my shoulders," Miss Hall interjected. "But, the lines I liked best were, 'I ain't never bin to whur this boat cum frum, I wuz borned and growd up right her nigh Chattanooga. I don't get out much, but I jist had to cum and see this hur boat. I've heered uf it a

heap.' I finally asked her if she had a family. She drew herself up and answered me proudly, 'Yes'm I have raised
fourteen youngin's and nary a one uf ems ever been in
jail.' Isn't that precious? I wouldn't have missed my conversation with that dear mountain lady, so genuinely
proud of her family, for all the city sights. That's to me the
unique charm of these trips on the boat. I've met all kinds
of people, but none can surpass that quaint dear soul I met
today."

I had to agree with Miss Hall, a Vassar educated lady,
who could appreciate so many things, even the fact that
Mrs. Mountain Lady had so many children and "nary a
one had been in jail." That seems like an achievement,
expecially now.

: 15 : DOCTORS AND SANDBARS

THE QUESTION OFTEN arises, "What type of people ride the *Delta Queen?*" The answer is, "It depends on what trip you're talking about." The shorter the cruise, the younger the crowd. Normal-sized families seem to manage the cost of a three day to one week's cruise without a strain on the family budget.

A seven-day Kentucky Lake cruise attracted persons who have a two weeks' summer vacation from a secretarial office, or teachers off from school, many couples on a much needed time away from their small children while "Grandma" takes over, or some older persons giving their grandchildren a treat. But as a rule, the highest percentage of river travelers were those past the halfway mark of life or even into advanced age. It is an easy, relaxed manner of travel, and attracts those who seek rest, a slow pace of life, and time to enjoy what they see. There are a great number at the other end of the line on all cruises however, seeking a bit of romance and lively activity.

The variety of people and their health status made it a policy for trips of ten days to three weeks duration never to be started without a ship's physician on hand in case of emergency. Special rooms were set aside for his professional use, and for storing his medical equipment. We had a few semi-retired physicians on whom we could rely to help us out, and very often they would request a choice of certain trips far in advance. On one occasion I recall, or rather shall never forget one who was a newcomer. His predecessor had recommended him and had explained to him in advance, "Just go along and be there with your equipment: you'll enjoy it. You won't have a whole lot to do but you'll get a free trip—one you'll always remember." He was certainly right in this last statement.

The trip north to Pittsburgh was calm and uneventful. I was on board one-way north and reported to Dick Simonton, our majority stockholder since 1958, "Dick, everything is going great. All seem happy and not a thing to worry about. Our new purser-steward combination seems okay and since the chef is so very dependable, the food is always fine. Martin just seems to be improving all the time and I am well pleased."

Dick concurred, and seemed to be thoroughly enjoying his trip to Pittsburgh. I flew home on Sunday, the next day after the boat landed, gratified at the smooth way things were running.

About three o'clock in the morning three days later I received a phone call from the purser.

"Mrs. Greene, we have had a little trouble. There was a knifing in the cook house tonight, and Martin and one of the other cooks were pretty badly hurt. Both are in a Parkersburg hospital. We'll have to make some kind of arrangements for help when we get back to town." News like this in the middle of a hot summer night is a little disquieting.

He added, "We'll have to get another bartender, as he's off too. Police got him for drunkenness in Marietta." It looked like all hell had broken loose.

When I met the boat on the following Sunday night, at lock number thirty-six as she neared Cincinnati, everything looked all right. One of our good waiters had taken over the job in the bar without trouble, a position which he was to hold for the next six years. The kitchen tragedy proved to be more serious however, and we started a search for another chef in the middle of the season. Also a purser, for shortly afterward that one handed in his resignation on a three day notice.

I wonder how we got through that season without faithful Martin and his helper. It passed somehow, with others stepping in to take over, and few passengers ever knew the change had occurred.

Dr. Hudson realized how right Dr. Scott had been when he told him "It'll be a trip you'll never forget," for Dr. Hudson said, "I haven't had so much excitement and bloody work since Saturday nights of my internship at General Hospital."

Another dear doctor, who was retired, served the boat often. He was professionally capable, and always knew when to throw in a funny remark. As years began to pile up however, he advised us that he felt he could no longer perform his duties on the boat—his heart couldn't take the stairs—and he added, "I'm fast approaching the age where all I seem to remember is that I've forgotten something." He went on, "You know Tom, there's various stages of growing old. First you forget names, then you forget faces, then you forget to pull the zipper up and then you forget to pull it down." Although he was speaking in a humorously exaggerated manner, he was quite aware that a younger man should take his job. Dear Dr. Schoolfield.

Once, when I met the boat in Madison, Indiana, Dr. Scott entertained me with a funny episode which had occurred during the trip.

"Mrs. Greene there was a young couple on here—oh, maybe forty, that's young to me—came from upstate somewhere. Don't think they'd ever had a drink in their life. Well, being on vacation away from home, they'd turned loose and couldn't handle it very well. The Captain called on me, for the man was sick, and his wife was wild. I'm telling you, it was the funniest thing I'd ever seen. The husband finally went to bed to sleep it off, and she was undressed but decided to go out on deck.

"Well she was running everywhere, wearing nothing but her husband's dinner jacket and throwing her arms around everyone she saw. We had a time calming her down. When she finally got settled down in her room we didn't hear another word out of them till the next day. They were the most embarrassed couple you ever saw when they found out what a spectacle they'd made of themselves. The captain tried to console them: To make them feel better he said to her, "Now don't feel bad, we understand; you know we've all done that sometime or other." Dr. Scott slapped his knee and whooped and hollered, and added "They got off at Henderson, Kentucky and went home, they were so ashamed. I actually felt sorry for them."

It is interesting to observe people on vacation away from home. They will often venture into situations they'd never dare to in their own community, where they are well-known and highly respected. As I have often repeated, the boat is all things to all people.

So many passengers have remarked to me, "My, it must be fun owning a business like this, and riding up and down the river all the time." Little did they realize what went on backstage to keep the show going. The part passengers see is only the tip of the iceberg showing above the water.

On most cruises, if I heard the whistle blow in the middle of the night for a landing or a lock, or felt the boat bump the wall, when I stopped to recall what day it was and looked at my watch, I could very accurately tell where we were. One night it was a bit different. About three a.m. I awoke, turned on my transistor and was amazed to pick up the pilot on the *Delta Queen* talking over his communication system to another boat—a freak connection.

"Well now heah, I'll tie up theah on to the stabbard side and shove ya off it, if I kin," came from the other boat.

"Okay, I'll be mighty glad, she's stuck like hell here on this sandbar."

"Now as soon as we're all fast I'll come ahead on her and hope she'll budge." The boat didn't move. The voices seemed to be picking up interest in the project, so I threw on a robe and slippers and slipped out to see what was going on. She was stuck all right, on a sandbar. All the horsepower that could be summoned wasn't doing any good. For hours they worked: pulled, pushed and tugged, until I heard the other pilot in his "cajun" accent warn, as he gave a particularly hard drive, "Cap, I don't want to knock a hole in 'er." Soon the boat gave a lurch and we were free again. Just one of the many times the sand was just too enticing for Her Majesty the *Queen*.

Sandbars on the river have been a problem since the beginning of the steamboat era. Before the building of locks and dams it was not uncommon for boats to be stuck for hours, days or weeks in low water stage. After the canalization of the Ohio River, however, which was celebrated in 1929, a nine foot channel was assured, except under unusual circumstances. Most of the original locks in the Ohio were the type that held the water back by means of wooden wickets hinged to a device at the bottom of the river. In high water these wickets were tripped by especially equipped small maneuver boats, dropping them to the river's bed. The water then flowed freely over the top creating an "open river." If the flood stage was of long duration, mud and silt formed on top of these wooden wickets making it difficult for the maneuver boats to pull the wickets back to their upright position.

If the work proceeded too slowly, the water rushed out too fast, creating a hazard by exposing sandbars which were normally submerged There are also sandbars at the mouth of most tributaries of the Ohio River which the pilot carefully avoids, as they are well marked by well placed buoys.

The ever shifting sands of the lower Mississippi were unpredictable, and while low water stage usually prevailed in autumn, the Delta Queen has been known to get stuck in floodstage between Cairo and New Orleans. This bit of inconvenience was excitement to the passengers, especially when it became necessary to engage the help of another boat to pull us off. No serious damage was ever done; however, the sand which was stirred up invaded the plumbing system of the Delta Queen, creating a lot of extra duties for the engineers and maintenance men, who in turn cussed under their breath at the pilot or anyone who could be blamed for this inconvenience. Toilets would flush on and on, requiring the service of a plumber before shutting off; and muddy water was a nuisance for hours.

The Delta Queen barely escaped another unwanted delay when in 1967 she left Cincinnati bound for New Orleans: weather fine, and all was well. The river rose while she was gone. At New Orleans we received news that a group of barges had broken from their mooring above Markland Dam, below Cincinnati. They had floated pell mell down to the big dam and ploughed into the lock chamber and wickets. Navigation was at a standstill until repairs could be made. Since wickets were damaged, the river was losing her pool fast.

The wharf boat at Cincinnati, some thirty-five miles upstream was left high and dry on a mud hill, and had to be pulled and yanked by harbor boats for hours before she was cleared. Down the river forty tow boats lined up below and above Markland Dam waiting their turn to go through when navigation resumed. The *Delta Queen* was on her way upstream from New Orleans and the last wicket had been repaired and put in working order only a few hours before she arrived. All the other boats stood gallantly aside and allowed the Queen to go first, through the lock chamber and on into Cincinnati on schedule, so that our passengers could get their early reservations for their return home. The Queen again proved she led a charmed life.

Another time we had just returned from a cruise to Chattanooga on the Tennessee River, where we locked through the wonderful high dams of T.V.A. fame. After we returned to Cincinnati, we heard that one of the locks had received damage to its lock chamber, which halted navigation in that area for months. We were lucky we were not trapped in the pool above the damaged lock, or we'd have had a long look at the red clay banks of the upper Tennessee.

WHEEL TROUBLE

THE UNIVERSAL QUESTION asked by passengers aboard the *Delta Queen* in our lean years was, "Why don't you advertise more? We had a hard time finding out about this trip. Our agent seemed to have no information about it, but I'm surely going to tell him when I return home. It's been the best vacation I've ever had, and I've been all over the world."

Advertising meant money, so we aimed to channel our efforts in the appropriate directions. But often times we missed the smaller newspapers or the particular source which any one person may have had in mind. We sent brochures each year to the leading travel agents throughout the land, but sometimes a new clerk or other employee, who was not well informed on steamboat service was approached about a river cruise. Hence misinformation was passed along.

For this and any one of dozens of other reasons, the *Delta Queen* was not always well known to everyone. We had many sources of publicity other than paid advertising but evidently not enough. We had a good product to sell, and one that was unique, satisfying and popular with those who were lucky enough to learn about it and had a real desire to take our cruise. Much of our advertising was by word-of-mouth, by our satisfied customers who praised our service to their families and friends. It was a rare occasion for those who rode with us to leave unhappy or disgruntled. About twenty-five per cent of our business was therefore repeat passengers: some traveling each year, and some for as many as three or four or more trips per year.

People became friends on the *Delta Queen* cruises and when they returned the next time, they made special effort to join those they had met before. If only we could acquaint more people with our wares, we knew we'd make a sale, but it seemed to take earth-shaking events, producing monumental publicity, to put the *Delta Queen* squarely in the public's eye.

Finances were growing worse and worse. How much longer we could continue in the struggle to keep the boat going was questionable. January first of each year found us scrounging around to pay bills, keep our feet dry from flood waters, and get out on the first trips of the season—to New Orleans, and Mardi Gras in spite of ice threats and high water.

Our mortgagee was patient but ever anxious. We never failed to meet the interest payment on our loan, but to get the principal shaved down was a slow, serious process. Lengthy conferences were held and the situation became more threatening. There was little that could be done in the matter, it seemed. Boats don't sell like homes, and the few opportunities which were presented to us were never satisfactory. All my friends advised me, "above all else don't put your own private funds in that boat business in order to save the day. Let it go down the drain first, if necessary." I hoped it wouldn't be necessary and it wasn't, but there were some very close calls.

In 1957, the *Delta Queen* left for Mardi Gras with a good paying trip. I left with the boat going one-way south to New Orleans to see how things went, as was my custom. There was the usual big crowd of well-wishers down to see the boat off, much gaiety, and bon voyage parties. At the moment of departure streams of confetti were tossed and draped overboard with a tumult of good-byes waved from deck to shore.

The *Delta Queen* had not progressed far downstream before a definite note of difficulty was noticed by the crew, most especially the engineers department, in addition to persons on shore. Since I'm not an engineer, nor particularly mechanically minded, the situation was puzzling as to cause, but the effect was that the big paddle wheel which propelled the boat along rolled in a loppity-lop fashion each revolution. To an observer it seemed that the wheel started the revolution in a well meaning, strong, healthy manner, but lost heart and strength as it reached the peak of its stroke. It halted, nearly stopped, reconsidered, took a shot of adrenalin, and rushed madly on for the remainder of the revolution, firmly resolved to make amends for its half-hearted beginning. But then it would repeat the uncertain revolution another time.

This uneven performance could be detected by all whose ears and eyes were trained to listen and watch for this sort of trouble. A comparable irregularity, if heard through a doctor's stethoscope on the human body, would result in a prescription for lengthy bed rest with strong medication and care.

The lock master at the dam called out to us over the communication system as we passed swiftly over the submerged wickets in open river, "What's the matter with you all? Broke down or something? Wheel's not acting right." We were an open target for the trained eyes of the lock master as we loppity-lopped downstream.

The captain spent much time in the engine room in consultation. The engineer was less than verbose regarding the symptoms of the afflicted *Queen.* There always seemed to exist between engineers and pilots and captains a mutual "kid glove" type of rapport. Everyone seemed to hesitate to push his luck in criticizing the engineer's performance, for he was master of his domain. Who else had sufficient knowledge of the intricate machinery of a steamboat to keep her in balance and good working order at all times? He was the diagnostician, surgeon, nurse and dispenser of all that was necessary for a healthy steamboat's innards. None could question that it was a highly specialized job. If a pilot hit the lock wall too hard in an onshore wind or got out of the channel and scraped the boat's entire length over a buoy, everyone knew it. Even the layman could have an idea of the error, and the pilot would get his verbal comeuppance, but very few people could question an engineer's knowledge of what mystery might exist in the engine room.

This time the chief didn't seem to be too greatly interested in what the trouble might be. He seemed even less interested in correcting it. As a matter of fact he was sick, and confined to his room, leaving the duties mostly to his subordinates. Our ship's doctor, who always seemed willing to help out in any emergency above and beyond the call of duty, volunteered to talk to the chief, improve his health if possible, and at the same time improve his mental attitude and disposition until the wheel problems could be corrected.

He talked long and seriously but his effort to get some positive action was fruitless. One of our pilots avowed that he had sufficient knowledge of the engineer's work to know what was wrong. But he was not about to overstep his protocol and take over the job. We lopped on down the river, the trouble growing worse each day, until it looked as if the wheel would soon give up the struggle and stop dead in its own wake.

We neared Greenville, Mississippi, where it was decid-

ed we should land and get help from an expert. By now all attention was focused on the wheel's condition. A rainy fog threatened the visibility more and more. In the dining room entertainment with music and dancing continued each evening, but each member of the crew was subconsciously thinking of something else. Mechanically minded men passengers strolled casually back to the engine room door to offer their opinions and advice to the already saturated minds of the second engineer and his helpers.

We at last put out a line and tied up to a tree, hoping to hail a passing towboat to come to our rescue and tow us into Greenville. Some further tinkering went on while we were tied up and the word came, from those who were supposed to know, that things were now fixed. We cast off the lines and floated into the current only to find that things were truly fixed all right. The wheel wouldn't turn in *any* direction. Marty Stouder, the hostess, and I were taking a minute off from the dining room's entertainment to stroll back toward the engine room, when a frightening gush of steam suddenly filled the engine room and drove us out in a hurry. Protocol be hanged, I thought. If anybody on this boat knows what's wrong and can do anything about it he'd better get busy. I knew how important the income of this trip was to our finances back in the Greene Line office, and if this trip flubbed up, things were going to be worse than anyone else suspected.

By now it was midnight and somehow they got a line out and tied up once more. I gave up. I left the whole unsolvable mystery to the master mechanical minds and took to my room and my prayers. A miracle seemed to be the only solution. I sensed the demise of our business unless help came, fast.

Next morning when I awoke, the sun was shining bright after the lifting of a heavy fog and the boat was paddling happily and smoothly down the muddy southern waters of the Mississippi. All fears were past. I learned that the ailing "cam" of the wheel had been properly adjusted after the amazing discovery that all prior efforts had been applied to the wrong side of the wheel. Somehow, my own common sense had told me that that was the case all along. I wasn't an engineer, just a "dumb woman" but President and General Manager. It was a happy day for the *Delta Queen*, she'd come alive once more, and traveled on into New Orleans where she tied up at the foot of Toulouse Street. The engineer was worse off then we know. He ended up for a long stay in a hospital in New Orleans, and engineers were hard to come by that could control the Queen of the Delta.

: 17 :　　　　　　　　　　TO CALIFORNIA
FOR A DEAL

FEBRUARY 13, 1958: The *Delta Queen* seemed to have at last come to the end of a dead end street. The recent dry docking experience had been too much for her to survive. Bills, more bills, no money to advertise, which meant poor prospects for any much needed revenue. The weather was bitter with zero readings on the mercury, and oil was fast being used up to maintain sufficient steam to prevent water pipes from freezing. We decided to quit. An announcement to this effect carried on both television and in the newspaper was followed by a deluge of interested speculators. Some wanted to buy her for a museum, others for a restaurant; some even had the idea of operating again on other waters. The phone rang constantly, letters piled high, and the weatherman's report was "Colder, zero tonight with floating ice in the Ohio River."

I returned Richard Simonton's check which he had sent as a deposit on a cruise for the next summer. This announcement that the boat had ceased operation hit him and his family hard. They had taken a week's trip the previous July and had gone home to North Hollywood with their four children in tears. Their only consolation was the bright prospect of returning for another cruise the next year.

As a result of several phone calls back and forth between Cincinnati and North Hollywood an agreement was reached to see what could be done to forestall this end to steamboat passenger service on the Ohio. Mr. Simonton and his family loved steamboats and he seemed interested in us. This interest must have been accelerated by the avid desire of his four children to get another trip on the river.

"Get on a plane" he said, "it won't cost you anything, and come on out. Let's talk this over. The weather is favorable for flying—I'll meet you. So, come along." I had never flown so far, nor had I ever gone on such an important mission. I discussed the matter with my children, other officers of our company and of course the holder of our mortgage who seemed like the ever present "wolf to come out of the forest."

I thought of so many dear passengers to whom the *Delta Queen* meant the greatest entertainment and bit of fantasy in their lives. She was beautiful, seaworthy and sound, having just passed a rigid inspection. Somehow a voice within me urged me on to do all I could to make it possible to continue operation. My family said "What can you lose? It's worth a try." Others in our company were not quite so encouraging, with "Let her go down the drain, can't come out ahead." I stood almost alone in the decision—certainly no assuring force encouraged me to "go ahead, you'll be okay, things will turn out well." Still, I decided to venture a trip to Hollywood. I packed my best suits, which were appropriate, wore my blue cashmere coat with custom made hat to match, borrowed my daughter Mary's Stone Marten neckpiece, and boarded a plane headed west, truly a "Babe in the Woods."

As we approached Los Angeles National Airport I thought I had never seen such a vast expanse of lighted area. It looked like hundreds of thousands of miles of city lights. As I walked down the concourse at the airport, I spied Dick Simonton and a friend Bob Wittenberg, all fresh and well-dressed. It was only eight-thirty there but in my book it was nearer midnight and I felt every minute of it. A surge of near panic encompassed me for a brief moment, but there was nowhere to escape. I braced up and clipped bravely on.

I found them both very cordial, but within my own mind I kept thinking, "Gee these are Hollywood people, they know nothing of my river steamboat problems, and haven't any conception of what the real issue is. I mustn't dupe them, 'sell them a bill of goods' or in any way trap this fine well-meaning man." He looked so young and I felt so old.

I was deposited at a very desirable room at the Hollywood Roosevelt Hotel, which was like a dream world. Bathers were enjoying the pool outside the patio of the Hotel. What a contrast to the Ohio River and its floating ice and zero weather, which I had left behind only hours ago. I found myself in the position of simply remaining comfortable in the luxury of the hotel, except when Mr. Simonton would call to take me to lunch, dinner, or to sit in his office and listen to his business day activities and to discuss steamboats. I soon discovered he was a busy man, active in the fields of television, radio, and Muzak recordings, all of which sounded strange to me.

What a far cry from "She's going to zero again tonight. If we don't get some break in the weather the oil's going to run out and she'll freeze to hell. There's more bills coming in and these new folders are going to cost. Oh, there must be a better way to make an easy living."

I met more new people. The elegant home of Mr. Simonton was a pleasant place to be on Valentine's Day, with everyone receiving a greeting of the day at his or her dinner plate. The cordial maid and butler were like one of the family. I was all ears and eyes. On the second night at dinner, out of town guests were present. Mementos of the boat were used for dining room decorations, recordings of the boat's music were played over a stereo, and a model of the boat served as a centerpiece for a real *Delta Queen* atmosphere. Yet, so far, no definite commitment had been offered to help us out of our financial difficulty.

I bided my time in wonderment, careful not to appear too pushy or anxious. After all, he had called me to come out there, and I did want it to be his desire to get into the turbulent boat business rather than being pushed into it through high pressure salesmanship. I feared he was a bit unaware of what all was entailed. They were such wonderful, hospitable people. It seemed incredible that someone in such a different world could be faintly interested in our river business with its many "ifs" and hazardous probabilities.

On Sunday I was their guest to see a rehearsal of the Dinah Shore television show. I was scheduled to return next morning and yet no mention of I'll give you 'X' dollars for 'Y' stock in your company. I was getting itchy. After a lovely dinner at the Beverly Club on Sunday night, Mr. and Mrs. Simonton and I drove to his office, and went in to have a long "down to where the rubber meets the road" talk. I assured them they were not buying a picnic. But as a conclusion to this summit conference, Dick Simonton took out his check book and started writing. I deposited the welcome check safely in my purse, hardly believing it could be true.

This was the beginning of a better than ten years association which was to be full of turbulences, rough gales, but profits and happy times as well. I came back to Cincinnati via Chicago the next day, to zero weather, my ailing boat, and all those who discredited the whole idea of "Saving the *Delta Queen*." Those very words were to become almost a household phrase in the near future, for we soon were back in business. This was the beginning of a new era with more to come. Dora Schrieber, a faithful St. Louis passenger, had not bought her new mink stole in vain. "The boat will run again," as she optimistically predicted all along.

Business picked up at Greene Line upon my return from California. My daughter-in-law Caroline Greene again took charge of the reservation desk and we all pitched in—busier than ever before, in a rushed effort to get our brochures out and into the hands of the travel agents. Even the night watchman offered to help "stuff" folders in his spare moments. An immediate announcement that the *Delta Queen* would resume her regular schedule in April of 1958 was surely welcome news to her many friends everywhere.

Repair and paint jobs were soon under way, for the *Queen* now had a new lease on life and must be all gussied up in her finest garb in readiness for her kick-off spring cruise. There was soon an upsurge in our business, the momentum of which is still felt today. Every interested person must have figured that they must get that long planned river trip in before some other unknown and unseen malady struck Her Majesty down, and steamboat trips for the *Queen* would end forever.

: 18 :   A STOWAWAY

A TRIP TO THE Kentucky Derby aboard the steamboat *Delta Queen* was exciting and expensive. A passenger could enjoy his own hotel afloat on the overnight cruise from Cincinnati to Louisville, and awaken next morning within an easy fifteen minute bus ride to Churchill Downs. After a lively day at the race track, he could return to the relaxing atmosphere of the boat and enjoy an early May Saturday night boat ride back to Cincinnati, arriving the next afternoon. From here by means of a cab, or his own safely parked car, he was soon on his way home. It was a good arrangement for those affluent enough to afford it.

The Derby crowd was special. Many business executives generously entertained special customers in this manner. Other parties were merely out for a gala weekend, and a few had budgeted their funds especially with this trip in mind, where they could enjoy a swingin' crowd, and be able to boast of their one trip to the Derby. In 1959 this trip offered a special thrill.

All afternoon deck hands had busily wielded their broad brooms over the vast expanse of concrete deck of the Greene Line wharf. All junk scraps of iron, empty soft drink cases and bottles were stacked away, hidden from sight. Steps and railings leading up to the Greene Line offices were decorated with a fresh paint job. The wharf-boat watchman clipped along with an unusual spring in his step, wearing a "store" jacket, which he reserved for such auspicious occasions. His face was freshly shaven, and his scanty, receding blond hair was slicked down over one side in an attempt to conceal his bald spots. He took great pride in directing the parking of the passengers' cars, as evidenced by his Sunday best appearance, even though it was Friday.

On board the boat, the maids had extra "in-port" help. Staterooms were scrubbed, beds equipped with crisp linens, and mirrors shone. The whole place smelled of fresh readiness.

Porters and extra clean-up men had polished brass throughout the boat until door knobs shone like the luminous glow of the five o'clock sun on the Mississippi. The freshly waxed and polished floors were stripped with long paths of heavy brown paper to keep down the tracks of those crew members whose duties led them over the newly cleaned floors.

The fat, black chef wearing a tall white cap and newly laundered jacket, waddled a little faster as he stored great trays of homemade rolls in the walk-in refrigerator for use at the appropriate time. Dozens of filet mignon steaks and pineapple-decorated, sugar-coated hams were tenderly stored in the cavernous meat box for tomorrow's dinner. Pots and pans glistened, and the floors were spotless.

The Derby brought ball park prices and nothing was spared to provide the best of everything for the guests.

Even a stranger on the boat could sense the fact that this was a special day.

During the afternoon, the mate had been bothered by a scraggly appearing stranger who strolled around the wharf followed by a small white furry dog. His manner seemed aimless, and he gave no suitable answer when asked his name or what his business was at the wharf. Twice during the afternoon the mate saw fit to "run 'im up the hill."

After the mate finished his supper, about six o'clock,

he wound his weary way to his quarters on top deck to enjoy a much needed six hours rest and sleep before coming
on watch at midnight. He neglected to warn the captain of
his experience earlier with the tramp-like stranger.

At 6:30 p.m. the caravan of cabs and private cars began to file onto the dock, unloading the Derbyites. Sporty
appearing groups filed on board until soon the registration
line extended from the office window, along the cabin deck
to the top of the entrance stairway. Cadillacs, Buicks and
Mercedes Benz with license plates from at least twenty
states were assigned their special parking stalls which they
would occupy for the next two days. Sweating porters, lad-
en with expensive luggage pocketed tips unlike those on
any other cruise, as they politely escorted their customers
to their various staterooms.

Soon "All ashore that's going ashore," sounded from
the public address system. A noisy bustling of farewells between our guests and visiting friends was followed by a
louder "All gone" from the Captain on the bridge.

The big red paddle wheel backed around toward the
Kentucky shore, a short blast signaled that the boat was
leaving the harbor, as she nosed her bow downstream and
headed for Louisville.

The shrill calliope zinged its carnival notes into the
steel girders of the suspension bridge in a musical approxi-
mation of "My Old Kentucky Home" as the boat skimmed
underneath, sending waves undulating to both shores.

On board, the place was jumpin'. Waiters ran into
each other carrying out orders to rush buckets of ice to
Parlor J, a telephone company president's party. He was a
regular annual Derby customer and good tipper. An order
of twelve martinis and six Manhattans, plus a tray of hors
d'oeuvres to top deck for a party of insurance executives
from New York. . . . The deck steward puffed and
strained, as he carried a load of deck chairs to the head of

the boat for a group of writers from several important newspapers. Surely a good story would come from this group. With so much activity on board, almost any unusual event could have gone unheeded by those on deck.

The clerk was seated at the office window to answer questions and settle any problems which might arise while the purser was in his inner office in seclusion with a huge ledger "writing up the trip."

"Calling #47, Calling #47, please come to the purser's office," came out loud and strong over the microphone. This was the carpenter's number, and he responded at once.

"That couple back in Parlor M say they can't regulate the air conditioning. It seems to be whistling a tune."

The clerk gave the carpenter a sly knowing smile.

"Okay, I'll see what the tune is," replied Smitty.

He returned shortly with a sizeable wad of cellophane in his hand. "The last person in that room must have filled the opening with this, and it was whistling all right."

A spontaneous guffaw followed and no further trouble from that room.

Another call: "Number 25 please come to the purser's office, Calling #25." Soon a porter appeared.

"Bobby, go with a bucket and mop to the upper lounge—water is pouring from the ceiling, the deck watchman says." Some member of the crew had forgotten to close the shower curtain and water had splashed out onto the floor above, giving a good unexpected bath to the carpet beneath.

Soon the second cook appeared at the window with "Say, have you got a bandage? I cut my finger on a knife. The chef surely has them 'son of a bitches' sharpened up, just like razors."

The clerk opened up a special door which was filled with bandages, sterile gauze, kaopectate, milk of magnesia, spirits of ammonia, Mercurochrome, rubbing alcohol, and various other emergency medical items. A ship's physician once advised the purser, "Always have a pain killer, a stopper and a starter on board at all times, and a few stimulants in case of snake bites."

"I'm sorry about that, Jimmy, we'll get it all fixed up here now in just a minute." The purser left his important duties of the inner sanctum to give this medical attention.

"Thank you, Mr. McCann, you always know what to do. I'll have to cut with the dull side of the knife after this." A he-cackle followed as he strolled on back the guard toward the back steps leading to the galley.

No one on board had taken heed of a little scraggly man wearing a broad brimmed straw hat as he gingerly picked his way along the decks toward the engine room just before the boat left port. In his arms was a small white dog, which he soon deposited on a small ledge beyond the dining room and ordered to "stay". I doubt if the pet had graduated from obedience school but still he slept all evening on the ledge, guarding his master's hat.

Soon the stranger confidently entered the dining room, walked up to a busy waiter and said, "Say, would you do me a favor? I came on here with a bunch of friends and I'm going to have some fun. I slipped away from the crowd, changed into these old clothes and if you'll loan me a fresh waiter's jacket, it'll just fix me up for a joke I want to play on the others."

Fred Davis, the waiter, stopped, thought for a minute, looked him over suspiciously, then added, "Oh, yeah? Shuah. Right this way please, Sah." He always aimed to please the customers, and had learned that after the third martini, anything could be expected out of a Derby passenger. Fred graciously produced the jacket from the linen closet, accepted a ten cent tip and went on about his busy evening's work.

The stranger donned the waiter's coat and proceeded to melt into the crowd, emptying ash trays and busying himself about the dining room. His act had been perfect so far.

At midnight the first mate awoke from his evening nap and sleepily made his way into the crew's dining room to get his usual cup of coffee before reporting for duty. As he shuffled into the dining area, he did a double take. There on a chair, at the very captain's place, sat the stranger he had chased away during the afternoon.

News on a boat travels with the speed of light. In no time a swift ray was transmitted to the purser's office, who by now was down to the XYZ's of his passenger registration list. He summoned the clerk, who was in process of munching on a midnight snack before going off watch and on to bed.

They checked the list of names, and looked over the little man whom the mate had forcefully guided to the office. No, there was no accounting for this intruder. He was a "stowaway".

The news soon reached the Captain just as he was settling down in his room to look over the evening paper before turning out the light for bed.

His orders soon came, however, loud and clear up to the pilot house. "Kelly, land 'er d'wn heah wherev'r you can get in, got to put a stowaway off the boat."

The newsy night watchman, by the time he made his next round had alerted every passenger and crew member within sound of his voice, of the excitement at hand.

"Gonna land down here and put a stowaway off the boat, be turnin' around here now in a minute," he added in his penetrating voice.

The passengers on deck lined up at the railing to witness this rare event, something they'd often wondered about—a stowaway on a boat. When the late bar crowd got the news through their foggy senses many started for the outside deck, with mint julep glass in hand, afraid they'd miss the excitement.

The boat turned, headed upstream, held her nose in toward the Kentucky shore, on past a corn field, and gently nuzzled into a mud bank where the stage could be safely lowered onto solid ground. The huge gangplank squealed and groaned as it was slowly maneuvered by the deck hands and held in place where the clay was cracked and dried from the hot afternoon sun. The spotlight lit up the stage just like Broadway. The mate escorted the little stowaway and his dog down the gangplank. For once he was the center of attention of all those around him. In the middle of the stage under the bright light, he stopped, doffed his hat, bowed low, and giving a broad toothless smile he called, "You all pick a winner now, have fun for me, I almost made it to the Derby."

A loud round of applause arose from the decks of the *Delta Queen* as the stowaway and his dog leaped from the end of the gangplank and disappeared into the night. Everyone almost wished he'd stayed on board.

The boat slowly turned around and her spotlight dimmed away as she splashed her way toward Louisvile and the races.

Every passenger on board would now have an entertaining story to relate to his friends at the next country club party back in Long Beach or Oyster Bay. But I'll bet the best tale was the story the stowaway had for his buddies on the levee when he got back to Cincinnati.

: 19 :   FUN ABOARD

MUCH OF THE fun of steamboating is embodied in the passengers the boat carries, and the crew which serves them. The *Delta Queen* carries a crew of approximately seventy-six: the licensed personnel occupied the room on sundeck forward, near the pilot house, and since there were more crew members than could be accommodated in this limited space, others were assigned to a group of rooms on cabin deck opening to the outside across the stern of the boat. This area got full benefit of the noise from the engine room, the swish of the paddle wheel, and was affectionately labeled by those who lived there as "skid row". Although these rooms were small, there were advantages. They were more private, and one could relax in a decent state of deshabillé outside the small cubicle and enjoy a cool breeze before retiring for the night.

The concessionaire, Happy Briscoe, a humorous, lovable, heavy-set woman of seventy also accompanied the organist at the piano in the evening for the first "set" of music. Later, when she was through with the day's duties, she could don a robe and slippers and stretch out in a comfortable blue canvas deck chair outside her room until the rhythmic splash of the paddle wheel lulled her into a hypnotic state of semi-consciousness before going to her bunk for a night's rest. If she wanted a late snack and didn't feel like descending the stairs to the pantry, she might use the night watchman, Bruce Edgington, as a messenger boy.

He punched a clock, according to Coast Guard rules, at specific stations, making a complete round of the boat every twenty minutes from ten at night until six in the morning.

Happy would call to the amiable watchman, "Brucie, will you do me a favor? Tell Mose to bring me up a ham sandwich, with a few pickles and potato chips. Cream, no sugar. I want to relax here and rest my feet before I go to bed."

"How zat?" He was a bit deaf, and he hurried a little closer and listened with one hand cupped over his ear. Happy would repeat her request a little louder with a faint suggestion of impatience.

"Okay, okay, Happy," he'd respond hastily. "I'll tell him when I get down there in about five minutes." Bruce was a trustworthy watchman of unknown age, who could be depended on in whatever capacity, above and beyond the call of duty, which might of necessity be assigned to him. He had been with the boat since her first cruise on the Ohio, and boasted of a long line of service on other boats in years past.

Soon Happy might be joined by the organist, Harmon Mize, who would be "taking five" to go to his room just around the corner, to remove his dinner jacket which he'd worn all through dinner and the evening's entertainment. Now that formalities were a bit more relaxed, he would soon go back down more comfortably dressed in his shirt sleeves to play for the dancing crowd until midnight. He sipped slowly at a cup of coffee, stopped to lean against the railing a minute and drawled in a Meridian, Mississippi accent, "This shuahly is a dancin' crowd, and the bahr is full. They had seventy-five hats to judge tonight. Damn, I played evah thing in the book befo' the judges could make up their mind."

"Yeah, and I'm selling stuff in that souvenir stand. I

think every grandmother on here took *Delta Queen* tee shirts home to her grandchildren. I'm clear out of size six and eight. I'll have to call Mrs. Greene to bring a supply of color slides to Madison, too. They cleaned me out of the ones of Oak Allee, and I'm taking orders. Want a piece of this sandwich? Mose must think I've been shoveling coal all day, and I feel like I have, but he's got too much piled on this plate. I can't get away with all this." She broke her sandwich in two, careful not to mangle it too much.

"Thank ya', just—oh that's plenty."

"Say, you know what I did the other day?"

"What did you do, Happy?" Harmon answered with an infectious bubbling laugh in anticipation of whatever incident her sense of humor might concoct, as he continued to munch on his sandwich.

"On my way back from the foot doctor's office—you know I spent a whole week's wages for those darned orthopedic shoes he fitted up for me. . . . Well, I sat down in the crew's dining room to eat some peaches I'd bought up town. I put the peelings in one bag and my shoes in another. Started to my room to put my shoes away—and what do you think? I carried the bag with the peach peelings to my room and threw the shoes in the river." A knee slapping laugh followed from both Happy and Harmon.

"Well Happy, I'm a son of a gun." More laughter from both.

"I just think I'll forget about the shoes, they looked like two gun boats anyway," Happy concluded. "Anyway the peaches were good."

"Oh, my time's up. I've got to get down there, have a request for a Virginia reel and that man from Atlanta, he's half tight, fancies he can sing and is just champin' to get to the mike to favah us with 'Moonlight and Roses.' I shut it off at the wall before I came up, but I guess I'll have to let him turn loose to keep him happy."

"Goodnight Happy, I'm really sorry about your shoes."
A spontaneous giggly laugh wafted back as Harmon disappeared down the stern stairway and made his way past the
engine room, through the bar and onto the dance floor,
where he started up "Turkey in the Straw" at the Hammond for a Virginia reel for the waiting crowd.

The crew's dining room was served by a "texas tender", a waiter whose only job was to attend to the needs of
the officers. Sometimes a waiter who for some reason was
not quite up to continued service in the dining room,
would find himself serving the officer's table. Mose was
loved by all, had been with Greene Line for thirty years,
and was quite deaf. For this reason he was maintained as a
faithful texas tender. The crew members developed a new
language all their own. It was called "Mose English."

Mose would call out loudly, as most deaf persons do,
"Do you want chicken or ham?"

The young clerk would curve his elbows akimbo and
flap them like two wings. That meant "chicken!"

The second cup of coffee was signified by pantomime,
the pouring from an imaginary coffee pot into the cup
which sat by one's plate.

A request for milk was the imitation of milking a cow.

To indicate that one was finished eating and the plate
should be removed, both hands went up and out indicating "Take it away."

Often times a verbal attempt was successfully made to
convey an order to Mose.

One watchman had a difficult lisp in his speech. "Oxtail soup today. Want soup, Sammy?" Mose queried.

Sammy lisped loudly, "No, no Mothes, I don't want
no hot 'tailed' thoup." Then he'd turn to the others and
confess, "Mothes can't hear and I can't thalk. Thath a hell
of a note." One had to nurture a sense of humor, and no
insults ever resulted.

The captain would shout, "Mose how did that ghost sound that night in the Shiloh Cemetery up at Pittsburgh Landing last trip?" Mose with a twinkle in his eye would reply, "Just like this Captain, I heard him, all right— clomp, clomp, clomp," as he stamped loudly across the floor, a half hidden smile on his face, pleased and aware of how he was entertaining us all.

"Rabbit", another texas tender, who served us at times, was once caught, to his embarrassment primping and straightening his bow tie in front of a mirror in the dining room, as he waited for the dinner gong to sound. All dressed up in a fresh, stiffly-starched waiter's coat, he shyly turned aside and said "Ah, shucks, I jest look like a fly in a glass of buttermilk."

Another time, Rabbit was giving some "on the job" training to a new young employee who was to serve the Captain's table. "Now don't you let anybody see you wiping the chairs with the same cloth you wipe silverware with." I don't think the steward or captain heard the remark. I didn't—it was relayed to me by another crew member.

On a steamboat, dessert is referred to as "what's behind the door." A new, fresh-on-the-river, texas tender, unfamiliar with river terms, looked amazed and puzzled when the first mate bellowed "Say, Buddy what's behind the door today?"

The young man looked confused, turned around twice and upon looking behind the pantry door to see, said, "Sir, a broom and a mop." Even the other waiters enjoyed that unforgivable blunder.

A chef once was interviewing a young helper who wanted a job as second cook on the boat: "Okay, tell me first, how does you make your Jambalaya?"

The young man, unfamiliar with the term, and fumbling for an appropriate answer which would not reveal

his ignorance and ruin his chance for the job, finally came
out with, "Well, Boss, first I peels my potatoes." The chef
listened no further. He said, "Son, hand me down that 'spidah' theah." (Spider was river for "skillet.")

The chef struck this intruder into his world a good
blow where it did the most good, with the iron 'spidah'
and ran him up the hill. Jambalaya is a sort of dry Spanish
rice dish, containing no potatoes, and no steamboat cook
was considered worth his salt who couldn't serve good Jambalaya.

At eight each evening a phonograph record sounded
out over the P.A. system signaling the hour for the entertainment in the dining room to start. All who were to join
in the festivities trekked down the stairs in search of a good
table around which to sit nightclub fashion, in the huge
area which served not only as dining room but game room,
dance floor and a general place of assembly. A cocktail
lounge immediately to the starboard side at the stern of
the dining room was a convenience to those whose thirst
demanded a beverage. Live music was furnished for dancing, which followed a planned program directed by the
hostess. Sometimes it was bingo, other times a series of
games and contests. One which was always popular was the
game in which the entire room teamed off on two sides
each with a chosen leader. This was known as the "Army
and Navy" or "Battle of the Banks" (both banks of the river) or at times called "Baseball."

Many novel games fell into this evening's program.
The "Lemon Race" was always a good icebreaker. Each
leader chose six from his team to line up, ladies and gentlemen alternating. A nice fresh lemon was then passed
from under the lady's chin to the gentleman's chin without
touching the lemon with the hands. The positions the contestants would often be forced to assume in their rush to

win were hilarious. It usually brought the house down in laughter to see these passengers, many past middle age, indulging in such foolishness and having their first real unsophisticated tear-producing laughter in years. Then perhaps a boy and girl from each team would be blindfolded, seated flat on the floor and provided with a heap of silk stockings. The idea was for the boy to put as many stockings on his lady partner's leg as he could while he wore gloves and was blindfolded. The most dignified deacon would have to hold his sides with mirth at this procedure. On and on, just silly innocent merriment but good for the stale or worried mind and heart.

Another night there would be a hat contest, an event which took up the day in preparation. There were prizes awarded for the funniest, most original, most beautiful, and other special categories. Judges were chosen from the passenger list. Their job was difficult, for oftentimes the creativity and imagination of the contestants displayed real talent.

Then there was costume evening which served to bring out the imagination of all contestants. Generous prizes were passed out to all the winning contestants. The passengers treasured these trophies, which became conversation pieces when their owners returned home. This we realized was great advertisement for our boat.

Our able organist would furnish a real beat for dancing for the remainder of the evening, with vocal music, and passengers often joining in informally. There was a Virginia reel and "Paw Paw Patch." All were great fun and furnished good exercise for those who hadn't taken a hike around the deck or gone uptown at the last shore stop. On some trips the place was jumpin' till midnight; other trips, the crowd dispersed early and went outside to enjoy the cool evening breeze or a priceless moonlight night on the river. Others perhaps played cards, or read; everyone could follow his own inclination. There was always the late bar crowd, as well as the before dinner drinkers, a group which usually came in about five-thirty after a restful afternoon which included, for most, a short nap. The ladies dressed up fancifully in their dinner dresses, hair well coiffured, gentlemen freshly shaven and wearing dinner jackets or business suits, with scarcely a revealing wrinkle from having been packed all the way from California.

Of a passenger list of two hundred, there were often fifty or more from the West Coast, many of whom were regulars, returning one or more times each year. We had river friends all over the United States and many foreign countries. There was scarcely a town from Pittsburgh to New Orleans where my husband could not rely on some good friend to say, "Now, Tom, my car's out there if you need to get any supplies, or run an errand. It's all yours to use while you're in town" or "Can I take you up to the house awhile? I have a new boat model and some photographs I took last time I was on board. I'd like to show them to you." So it went—hospitality of the river and river friends.

There were many lighter moments with the crew: everyone had to create his own fun and surely did. Once a plastic dress figure from a ladies' apparel shop window was placed in the night watchman's bed with only the head exposed. Brucie came out of there yelling like an Apache, after he had sleepily started to bed after his long eight hour watch. Once he discovered what it was, however, he rolled it under the bed. Later, when the maid wielded a dust mop to clean underneath the bunk this body rolled out, giving her a good scare.

The accordion player once told the night watchman

there was a desperado loose in New Orleans. News had come over the radio that he was seen headed in the direction of Poydras Street where the *Delta Queen* was docked, dressed in a rain coat and carrying a music case which presumably contained a machine gun. Bobby donned the mate's rain coat, pulled the rain hat down over his face and darted furtively from one dark corner of the boat to another, carrying his accordion case, while the watchman made his rounds. This created no ends of laughs and teasing at the crew's table later. Brucie had been sure he had the fugitive cornered once behind the smoke stack and was about to attack him bodily with his two fists when he recognized his jokester, just in time.

The ship's newspaper consisted of one mimeographed sheet of information, news, and announcements which was placed at each plate at breakfast time. Each trip this literary gem carried a different name, which had been chosen by some passenger on the trip and for which a prize was awarded. The names were sometimes "The Queen's Diary," "Paddle Wheel Press," "Greene Leaves," or any other name a contestant might think of which would be fitting. On one occasion the engineer, who was a trifle deaf, passed through the press room (crew's dining room) after the prize had been awarded and called out: "Mary, what's the name of the paper this trip?"

"Why, let's see. Oh, 'Paddle Wheel Bits'. How do you like it?"

The engineer whirled around and shouted, "What? Paddle Wheel Bitch?!"

I'm sure he thought the insight of the passenger who suggested that name was uncanny. That's what he'd been calling the *Delta Queen* for years, every time a rudder was bent, or the water tank leaked, or the pump acted up, but he never dreamed it'd make the newspaper.

: 20 :

MUSIC, MICE AND
ROACHES

I'M SURE any restauranteur or handler of food, at times faces the dark forbidden subject of how to deal with invading pests, better known blatantly as roaches. They seem to follow any area where food can be found, and it's an ever present fight to keep any culinary quarters free of these detestable creatures. We took pride in the *Delta Queen's* high rating with the health authorities, but it was necessary to fumigate once or twice a year in order to keep down the influx of these crawling creatures. In spite of all the scientific devices known to man and science, by the end of the hot summer a few of these unwanted guests would have stowed away in the dark cracks and crevices, having been carted in presumably on the weekly supply of crates of wholesale vegetables. If the nightly spraying of insecticide had not succeeded in totally eliminating these crawlers, or if there had not been sufficient time between trips to spread the deadly cyanide, roaches would embarrassingly appear in the staterooms which were located nearest the food storage area. Once, on a late fall cruise under these unfortunate circumstances, a dear lady occupant of one of these rooms came to the purser and whispered in low tones, "I'm horrified, there are some strange bugs walking all over the floor of my stateroom."

"Oh, indeed! I'm so sorry. Well, I'll see the steward and perhaps he can do something about it. A spray should solve the problem."

Shortly afterward, the lady occupant of the adjoining room came to the purser with the same complaint, and received the same answer.

The steward summoned his best porter to get the deadly spray and use it in Room #1 immediately. The order was carried out with a renewed vengeance in this war against the bugs. The porter reported that they all disappeared, but they merely changed headquarters, crawled right over to the adjoining room and set up combined forces in some sort of protest march across the floor of Room #2.

Soon the lady in Room #2 came running to the purser with, "I do declare, I have a bigger supply than I had before, and you'll have to come and see to believe it. They seem to be doing some kind of a wild tribal dance." She caught the purser by the hand and led him cautiously on into her room. The purser in an effort to calm the occupant of Room #2 conjectured, "Oh, my dear, they're not dancing, they're writhing in pain, following their encounter with the spray. They'll soon be gone."

He then called the steward who took over personally. And, who knows, he probably used the best mode of destroying bugs known to man: place bug on paddle number one and strike with paddle number two. Such are the frustrating problems that sometimes confront anyone in the food business. We were relieved that this was the last trip of the season, and soon the boat would be devoid of people, a danger sign could be properly placed on the forward deck, the cyanide pellets professionally released inside the boat and every invading pest of any breed would immediately succumb in the deadly gas chamber.

Field mice often are known to enter one's home in the city or suburbs when cold weather begins to chill the night air, and more comfortable quarters are sought in the

warmth of the first session of the heating season. Sometimes these pests have been found on a boat, believe it or
not. They receive the same cold welcome as any other of
their ilk, but occasionally one may seek out a particularly
secure hiding spot and show itself on extremely inoppor-
tune occasions.

A good friend and passenger had after much insist-
ence, agreed to favor us with one of her professional rendi-
tions of arias from well-known operas. The boat was alive
with keen anticipation of the occasion. Rehearsals during
the afternoon had worked out well and the vocalist, as well
as accompanist, was well in tune and coordinated for the
evening's musicale. The room was filled with an eager audience by eight p.m. The star rustled into the room in her
long, low-cut, brocade evening gown, with a rose in her
hair well coiffured high on her head. The organist was ap-
propriately dressed in his formal attaire. The program
started.

Just as the vocalist was inhaling a deep breath, elevat-
ing measurably her high bosomed—head-on—appearance a
tiny mouse scampered from under the Hammond organ,
between her feet and on out boldly across the floor as
though he were part of the act. He halted as if to look over
the house prior to sending in his critic's report to the daily
ship's paper, turned left, and lost himself amid a scramble
of men, women and children all lifting their feet high, and
with the women holding skirts tightly around them. The
star of the evening, wrapped up in her rendition, and with
eyes closed, was ignorant of what had taken place and for a
brief moment interpreted the muffled outburst to be an applause for her performance, as she hit a high 'C' and held
it an incredible length of time. The organist likewise was
unaware of the bonus 'mouse act,' and was naturally
dumbfounded.

Not until they were both off stage and relaxed in the adjoining crew's dining room at the end of the show, were they told of what had taken place. It made headlines in next morning ship's paper. All took it in good spirit and I gained much respect for the wonderful disposition of these alleged "temperamental artists." They laughed loudest of all.

: 21 :   PILOT HOUSE TALES

THE TALES THAT have been expounded in a steamboat pilot house would amply furnish a television comedy series. This particular spot on a boat is secluded, high above all the decks and is always a place to get away from the crowd and have the most perfect vantage point to view the countryside and the river in all directions. There one can also view every activity on the open deck below. Extra pilots, necessary in areas where our own regular Ohio River men were unlicensed, were all colorful and interesting personalities. They loved to talk to anyone around to listen, for piloting can be a rather lonely job at times.

Conversations would go like this:

"You know once I was on a tow boat coming up the Mississippi River, just below Vicksburg. That tow was so big and heavy, it had to have two boats to shove it along. I was on one boat as pilot and the crew decided they'd play a joke on the crew of that other boat. A big black cat got aboard our boat somehow, and the engineer was so superstitious he wouldn't have the thing on board. So, you know the cook killed that cat, cooked him and sent him over those barges back to the crew of the other boat. Told them it was rabbit. The other crew ate it, didn't know any different, of course. And boy did they get mad when they found out the truth."

Laughter from the mate, clerk or whoever else was in the pilot house. "My God, that's awful. What did they do about it?"

"Well sir, a couple nights after that we laid up all night in fog. A damned hoot owl was up in a tree right at the bank where that other boat was tied up. The mate shot the thing; they picked its feathers off and cooked it, put nice gravy all over it and a few dumplings around, you know, and returned our favor. We thought it was chicken. Well, sir, I took one bite down through that thing's leg and it just split open like an old dry cedar log. I surely knew it wasn't the southern chicken I was used to. They sure got even with us."

The mate would say, "That reminds me of a time on the old *Katie Belle* when the steward figured he was doing mighty well. The store bills were way down and he wondered how come nobody ate any butter. Well, he came bolting into the dining room one night to see what was wrong with the butter. The damn stuff was rancid, nobody'd eat it, it was actually green with age. Well, that steward waltzes up to the captain and says, "Captain, how come you don't ever eat butter at this table? Is something wrong with the butter?" The captain took one look at that putrid looking pile of grease and said in his southern drawl, "Mistah Butteah answer him! You're old enough to speak for yourself." A burst of hearty laughter could be heard on the deck below.

"Say, you think it'll fog tonight, Cap?"

"No, there's a little wind starting up, and that lightning down there on the horizon looks like we might have a little rough weather here before long. It'll surely cool the air. I'd be mighty glad too. By the time the air conditioning gets to my room right under that hot roof, it's about lost its power. I thought I'd burn up in that damn room today. Guess we'll have to have that air conditioning unit serviced when we get in this week."

"Say, did you hear what happened on the boat last

trip? The steward had been missing some of his Delmonico
steaks, and couldn't figure who was gettin' away with
them. Ezra the deck hand had himself one of them dime
store straw suitcases full of something, and set it down
back in the boiler room. He let it set there until he had the
boat all tied up in port. Went back to get it and hurry on
home; got to the stage just ready to hop off and the bottom
fell out of that damn suitcase. Them frozen steaks had
melted back by the boilers, busted out of that suitcase and
slid all over the forward deck. They caught him red-hand-
ed all right. I tell you, what some people don't do."

"I bet he's not on there this week, after that stunt."

"Well, I'm goin' to go down and get a cup of coffee. Want me to bring you some?" said the mate.

"Yeah, and bring me a ham sandwich, too."

"Say, you know what Joe did last trip? He got a live alligator up New Orleans. You know, one of those little baby ones and he turned it loose in Brucie's room. The maid went in there to clean, gave one look at that thing crawling under the basin, and came out screaming. She says she'll never go near his room again, he can clean it himself. She don't want any ole alligator snappin' at her legs."

"Did I ever tell you of the time I was Captain on a tow boat down Green River? We were laid up in fog one night in at the willows, when the kitchen crew all decided to row ashore in a lifeboat and go in town. Well next mawnin' I came down to breakfast and they wasn't a thing to eat on the table. I said to the little texas tendah, "Where's breakfast, why ain't they any food?" He answered, "Why boss, the cook done got drown last night. We wuz comin' from town when a big ole snake fell off a willer branch down into the boat we wuz in, and that man lept overboard and never come up.""

"You sure have some strange experiences on a tow boat, don't you?"

"You sure do."

"This is WA 4141 calling lock number 51. Come in lock number 51. This is the *Delta Queen,* be up there now in a few minutes. That's mighty fine—we'll come right on up, a little windy but we'll make it. WA 4141 the *Delta Queen* to lock 51, ovah." The wind by now had begun to take on more velocity as the boat glided into the lock chamber.

The captain yelled from the bridge, "Come ahead

slow, get your possum in there. 'Eat 'em up'—up the river a little, there." A gentle bump as the wind blew the boat against the cement lock wall knocked the empty coffee cup from the window ledge; there was a loud crash as it hit the brass spittoon and the pieces rattled onto the floor. As the rain began to blow in, there was a great scurry to close the pilot house window. The lines were finally lassoed around an iron pin on the lock, and a welcome sound of "All fast" came from the bridge.

: 22 : CAPTAIN'S DINNER

THE CAPTAIN'S DINNER was a highlight of the last day of a cruise, and always followed a generous, lively champagne party.

The steward ordered a handsome floral centerpiece for the long table, which extended the length of the dining room. The chef and pantrymen did an extra special job of preparing a variety of tasty hors d'oeuvres. There was a huge bowl of fresh shrimp with a tangy delectable sauce dip, caviar, smoked oysters, sautéed chicken livers, the like of which I have never tasted elsewhere, fancy cheeses with special cocktail spreads and crackers, and dozens of other delicious dishes which appealed to smell, taste and sight.

The captain, the hostess and I, often accompanied by other officers or special representatives of the company, formed a receiving line and personally greeted all passengers as they entered the dining room. We all dressed in our best; evening or cocktail dresses were in order. This was the night for officers to don white uniforms heavy with gold braid and brass buttons. Dinner jackets, tuxedos or whatever else one had to "dress up" in were proper for the gentlemen passengers.

Cameras clicked with blinding flash bulbs, and the whole evening was a party to be remembered. Passengers caught a good camera shot of the long table of goodies before the onslaught of the consumers turned it into untidy disposables. After the champagne had been generously

served, or tomato juice in case there were any who preferred it, a toast was given by the hostess such as: "Happily
we have met, happily we have been, happily may we part
and happily meet again." Glasses were raised and often a
particularly appreciative guest would rise to the occasion
with a return toast, reiterating what a wonderful trip it
had been, lauding the captain, crew, hostess, owners and
each other. It became a mutual adoration society after a
few more glasses of champagne. The little lady whose physical infirmities had necessitated her descending the stairway backwards this night came down head-on. The cranky
man who had complained at Mardi Gras because the straw-
berries he was served were frozen, instead of fresh from the
vine, had a supply of compliments for the steward and
slapped him jovially on the back. The little woman from

the Bronx who had been mistakenly sold an upper in
Room 141 instead of a twin bed in Parlor A by her travel
agent back home, had an affectionate embrace for the purser. Now everything was fine. If the filet mignon steak was
too well done, or too rare, no one noticed it while the dinner music seemed to come more from the heart tonight, a
few waiters got carried away, and when time and space permitted, gave out between courses with a little levee "Hoe-
down" on the dance floor to the irresistable beat. The atmosphere was mellow with good will—"Yes, happily may
we part."

Passengers after dinner lined up at the captain's table
with their souvenir menu to collect autographs from all
seated there. We were always glad to give our signatures,
but I often wondered why they seemed so important to
everyone. Yet, in retrospect the value of these bits of me-
morabilia is focused more clearly, when I realize how rare
a steamboat cruise is.

After dinner, while conversation was still warm and
bountiful, it was relaxing to go on deck and watch the sun-
set behind the Ohio Valley hills, and drink in the pastoral
scenery on either side of the river. On up past Rising Sun,
Indiana, Rabbit Hash, Kentucky, and later Aurora, Indiana where a friendly whistle salute was given to friends living near Laughery Creek, and whose farm extended to the
river's edge. This hour of the day seemed a choice, precious
bit of time, just as the shadows lengthened into near dusk.
The last evening rays of the sun lit up the billowing clouds
in the west, and home was only a few hours away, with a
new crowd the next day to start all over again.

After the ship's concert was over that evening, we all
joined hands in a big circle and sang "Auld Lang Syne,"
which was followed by a "Hokey Pokey" as we danced on
into Cincinnati. Soon a stroll onto the forward deck would

show that the boat was getting excitingly near Cincinnati. Traffic on lower River Road became familiarly evident. The deck hands on the head of the boat set up a racket, jumbled and highlighted by banter and a few were singing. Sounds of a loud radio tuned to rock music, high-pitched, louder-than-usual voices and explosive laughter told me the deck hands, waiters, porters—in fact everyone —was anxiously awaiting that landing whistle. The *Delta Queen* would then soon glide alongside the wharf boat, bump it slightly as its watchman caught a handy line from our decks to pull the heavier manila lines in to tie up until next trip.

A few people stood near their packed suitcases ready to leave that night. Some, waiters, were ready to "hop her" ahead of the crowd as soon as she touched the wharf near the engine room door. A loud "Come ahead slow—Back her—come ahead a turn," followed by "All fast," sounded from the bridge. There was a whir of loud automobile mufflers, and the noise of taxi cabs bumping over the stage plank of the wharf, ready for service to the first customer. A traffic jam of cars on the dock, and crew members who were off-watch became landlubbers for a few hours. The purser hurried to get the mail from the Greene Line office on the wharf, and attended to last minute details before locking the ship's office for the night. I walked from the boat, waved goodbye to passengers lined at the railing who stayed on board until next morning, loaded my luggage into my parked car on the wharf and started for home, to see what was going on there. Another trip would depart tomorrow afternoon at three p.m. . . . .

: 23 :   SHIP'S CONCERT

ON THE LAST DAY of a *Delta Queen* cruise, the hostess was busier than usual, assembling all the available talent for an evening's entertainment for and by the passengers. Sometimes this proved to be a discouraging task, depending on how much outgoing personality and talents the crowd possessed. Often when a passenger was approached and asked whether or not he or she would participate in the show the answer was, "Oh, I can't do anything. I'll just watch."

It was at times a temptation, I'm sure, for a hostess to assemble everyone in the Orleans Room, and announce over the mike, "Now, Ladies and Gentlemen, we shall have the ship's concert, and since there was no one who felt he could perform, we'll all just sit and watch." This never happened, but sometimes the talent was sparse and volunteers few. Other times, the show could challenge an "Off-Broadway" production, or compete with a Gypsy Rose Lee burlesque.

There was always the rendition of the Lighthouse Keeper's Daughter, a one act drama, which depicted an old lighthouse keeper slowly climbing imaginary stairs to light the beacon which prevented ships from destruction in the treacherous ocean gales off Cape Hatteras. He was always murdered by a black-caped villian, who, after conking him over the head with a club, robbed him and disappeared down the long stairs and into the night, "never to be seen again." (Except when he took his bow at the end of the show) .

134

The sound effects of this club murder were always furnished by the organist lifting the piano bench lid, and dropping it with a sharp bang. Later, the plot thickened when the old lighthouse keeper's daughter discovered the tragedy and ran panic stricken to seek help.

When it was finally concluded by the doctor, along with the nurse, that "There ain't nuthin' I can do," the undertaker appeared, and all joined in to toss the old lighthouse keeper out of the window, as it was impossible to carry his lifeless body down the long narrow stairs.

Costumes and props for this fantastic production were quite individual and homely. A tin funnel with an attached jump rope served as the doctor's stethoscope, a black coat with tails, size forty, served for every undertaker regardless of his obesity. Consequently the sleeves were ripped and ill fitting. The cape which the villian wore hangs in my closet today as a memento, having once belonged to Captain Mary B. Greene as a dress-up wrap for the cool evenings on the boat.

The narration was usually carried out by the current hostess, with musical accompaniment, and all the acting was in pantomine. Each new cruise provided a fresh cast of performers, and the various bits of personal interpretation each character put into his part made our experience equivalent to seeing Hamlet played from Barrymore to Chamberlain.

Frequently, five or six of the lady passengers who were of suitable age, and, if not, were good enough sports to join in, formed a hula dance group, wearing colored grass skirts over a pair of colored shorts to match. A wide satin band would be tightly fastened around the bust area, with midriff and feet bare. Each dancer wore colorful crepe paper flowers in her hair, artificial leis, and rehearsed faithfully under the hostess' direction. She admonished the viewers always to keep their "eyes on the hands," in true Hawaiian fashion. The show opened with this chorus of South Pacific dancers.

On this particular trip, the leader of the hula line was a lady a bit past the age of beguiling maidenhood, but a good sport, ready for fun. When the organ started with "I want to go back to my little grass shack," the girls came wiggling out toward the center of the floor, on around in front of the crowd, dancing their slinky best. Just in the middle of the performance the lead dancer's strap broke— no doubt about it. The piece of red satin slid slowly and surely down, down, until it was almost to midriff—on one side. This was before the days of topless styles and even authentic hula dancers were properly covered in the right spots. She later told me, laughing in half embarrassment, "I didn't know what to do, but since I was the leader I just kept dancing. I figured the show must go on."

This extra strapless act brought the house down, for she made the best of her nude situation, but dreaded to face her more conservative sister who sat in the audience as one who was "just watching" and who was duly mortified by the outcome of her sister's part in the hula show.

One gentleman invariably recited "The Raven", and as he traveled with us frequently, the crew members and the social department got a bountiful exposure to this lengthy bit of Poe's works. On many trips another eighty-five-year-old gentleman, entertained for twenty-five minutes at the piano, with his many sheets of music placed methodically in front of him. Not exactly Carnegie Hall material but quite a feat: If I live to be eighty-five I'll do well to sit upright on a piano bench, let alone play the keys.

A high-pitched child's voice often came out loud and shrill over the microphone with "Found a Peanut" all the way from where he found it, ate it, got sick, died, went to heaven, got kicked out, went below, and burned his fingers shoveling coal. A fond mother always watched anxiously, and everybody clapped.

There was usually a *Delta Queen* chorus of men, women, or both, singing Barber Shop Quartet style and the trip was hardly complete until some older person recited "My get up and go has got up and went" with great feeling.

Occassionally we all stood in awe of a really talented passenger who generously shared his art with us at the piano, vocally, or in some other phase of entertainment. However, it was always a show by the passengers and for the passengers. They loved it.

It was the duty and desire of our various hostess' to see that all guests were thoughtfully looked after, from the very least inconspicuous passenger to the more outstanding ones. Each hostess over the years had her own special appeal and method of handling the public and each, from Esther Wohler to Marty Stouder was successful in her own way.

: 24 : GAS MASKS AT NATCHEZ

IN OCTOBER OF 1962 the *Delta Queen* prepared to leave for her late fall trip to New Orleans. Reservations were heavy, and the Indian summer was delightful. My daughter Mary and I decided to go along one way south and fly home. An interesting addition to the cruise was a crew of two photographers, a director, and an actress who doubled as a sound technician. They were making a film of the cruise for a television travel series.

Several other couples from the North Hollywood, California area were aboard: all rather important friends of our majority stockholder Richard Simonton. We were anxious to see that they all had a particularly good time. Our capable brand-new publicity director, Betty Blake, now vice president, was also on hand to see that everything contributed to good public relations. However, we were to be on our own after Evansville, Indiana, for there Betty was to take off for points west to attend a convention.

I could sense a slight tenseness among our crew and entertainment department. Could we keep this sophisticated crowd happy and interested on this old fashioned riverboat trip? Somehow, the steamboat's appeal seems very simple and folksy.

After the trip got under way, the filming was in session at any time and at all times. Long electric cords were stretched across the dining room in a desperate attempt to seek out a rare A.C. electric outlet. Bright, hot lights were placed at the right angle to avoid unnecessary shadows. The waiters picked their way around all this strange equipment, careful not to upset their enormous food-stacked trays onto a precious camera, and not to trip over a cord and fall headlong across the star of the moment. What goings on! Often I would be whisked away to the top deck to join in a particular shot, on the "sunny side" of the boat. The director timed the action just so, with orders to "Smile now, speak up louder, look this way—don't talk through your teeth, Susie." Of course it was exciting but perfection was demanded. This process lasted throughout the entire trip, but a wonderful film was thereby created, and it was shown all over the country. We were able to acquire a print to be shown privately or for advertising the boat.

South of Evansville on Monday afternoon, the Captain found ample time to give our passengers a half hour shore stop at Cave-in-Rock. A real pirate's cave, of natural origin, it was in earlier flatboat days the scene of outrageous crimes on the river. It was always a real surprise shore stop for the passengers whenever time and weather conditions permitted. The five o'clock October sun cast cool grey shadows through the hills, where the trees were covered with a galaxy of rust, maroon, yellow and brown leaves. A feeling of wistful nostalgia, mixed with a vague uneasiness came over me as I stood watching the deck hands tie the boat up to the shore. It was as if "something was in the air" but I didn't know what. Maybe it was occasioned by the thought of the long winter months ahead and the realization that another year of steamboating was almost over, with a long lay up stretched ahead of us: expense and no income. This year a dry docking was also on the *Queen*'s agenda, and that could mean 'most anything. Anyway, the strange feeling was there, and the light of the

setting sun as it shone through the autumn leaves seemed
to focus it even stronger.

A boom from the big silver bell on the roof signaled
departure time. The brief shore stop was over, and the passengers were slowly meandering down the path, having
had a look at the one noted pirate's cave on the Ohio River. The aroma of savory broiling steaks wafted up from the
general area of the cook house as the wind shifted upstream, and soon the chimes of the dining room invited all
to the first sitting of dinner. From the microphone "All
ashore that's going ashore," declared the Queen was ready
to proceed on her way. We said goodbye to Cave-in-Rock
for another year, hurrying down to the Orleans Room to
try out one of those steaks!

That evening, further downstream, our steward Ed
Gallagher stopped long enough while passing through the
crew's dining room to announce that trouble was brewing
in Cuba. President Kennedy had made some ominous
statements in which Russia and Mr. Khrushchev were
mentioned. This Ed had learned from his transistor radio
to which he listened avidly in order to keep in touch with
the world's activities. This bit of news struck a note of
doom in our hearts: the United States was sure to enrage
Mr. Khrushchev to the point where he'd send the bomb
over on the next plane. Then nothing, not even the film or
our distinguished guests would matter any more. Wednesday afternoon seemed to be the zero hour when action
might take place. But out on the river who would know?

If Brucie, the night watchman failed to pick up the
paper at the last town, no one could read the news, and
who had a radio or television?

Tuesday night we reached Memphis at midnight. I
crossed onto the dock and phoned my home to get the
pulse of things in Cincinnati. In this tense situation I was

torn between returning home from Memphis to fold my other chicks under my wings, or to stay on the boat come what may. I seemed to have an exaggerated idea of my capabilities in warding off impending disaster to any of my family wherever I happened to be. Even during World War II, I could remember dreams of an air raid with the sky full of falling bombs—I was always in search of my children or trying to protect them. The maternal instinct is unsuppressable.

After serious consideration I remained on the boat, and we pulled away from the Waterways Marine Dock in the early hours of the doomed Wednesday morning. Mary and I slept till noon; nothing terrible had happened, yet, so we descended to the crew's dining room for a lunch of bean soup, corned beef and cabbage, corn bread and collard greens. A real southern treat, but could it be our last meal?

Later in the afternoon I puffed up the steep steps to the pilot house to have a look at the mighty Mississippi from this coveted vantage point. The blue-grey, swiftly drifting clouds in the afternoon sky seemed to assure us that all was well, and in the peaceful atmosphere which one always enjoys in this secluded spot it seemed almost impossible to be apprehensive over anything.

Co-Captain "Doc" Hawley remarked in an offhand casual manner, "I guess Khrushchev hasn't done anything yet about our blockading Cuba." Somehow his nonchalance sounded reassuring. If we could just get past midnight and see the light of another day, maybe all would be well.

Wednesday night the show went along as usual. Marty Stouder, the ship's hospitable hostess had the crowd happy as always—our capable head of the entertainment department certainly knew how to get everyone right in the swing of Mississippi River steamboat life. Harmon's music

at the organ furnished a great inspiration for all the dancers. There was rhythm in the air and the cruise was a success so far.

We had just begun to relax when Thursday noon the boat gave her landing whistle for Natchez, Mississippi. Here our passengers would enjoy a much anticipated tour of the noted Ante Bellum mansions. As we pulled into the landing, a strange sight met our eyes. Instead of the usual sightseeing crowd which assembled at almost any port we visited, the landing was covered with soldiers. Had some drastic thing really happened, and we were under military rule?

We were advised by bullhorn that no one was allowed to go ashore until one of the National Guard officers came aboard. Everyone was ordered to assemble in the dining room. The rich lady from Santa Barbara quickly laid aside her needlepoint, the captain rushed down from the bridge, and the deck hand dropped his heavy line and stood aghast. In the dining area an officer of the National Guard demonstrated the correct use of a gas mask to everyone aboard the boat. No one was allowed to disembark and go uptown without his mask along.

We finally learned the cause of this unnerving scene: a chlorine barge had been sunk in the bottom of the Mississippi for some two or three years, and an effort was being made to salvage it. In case deterioration had been too much and the barge fell apart, the chlorine would be released into the water. This deadly gas would soon diffuse into the air, killing all within smelling distance who were unprotected by gas masks.

Natchez was filled with drab, olive-colored trucks and tents and National Guardsmen were everywhere. I wondered about pets, dogs, infants, and small children. The answer was, "Just wet a towel and hold it over their faces until safety is reached."

I could picture the horrible scene that would take place if the warning whistle blew! And so everyone walked up through the streets of Natchez or went on the bus tour of the lovely old homes carrying a dark olive-green tin case under one arm. Fortunately these cases were not used. Later as we passed on downstream where the salvage crew was working on a twenty-four-hour shift, we could actually see the tall cranes and maneuver boats, accentuated by strong spotlights and a terrific din. I think some people must have held their breath.

During the incident there were some interesting side lights. One of our deck hands was found in the middle of the night with his mask tightly fitted to his face. He resembled a Martian as he slept on his bunk, sweat rolling down his face. He was playing safe.

Another crew member reported having seen our pilot standing watch in the pilot house at three a.m. rigid and straight, with his mask tightly protecting him hours and miles after the critical time and place were past. At least this incident had taken our minds off the Cuban crisis, and we steamed into New Orleans on time.

Everything was back to normal, and even the filming continued. Our purser was in the limelight as he escorted the actress Susie through various spots in the Crescent City. They lunched in one of the well-known French restaurants, did the town on Bourbon Street—all for the television show.

What a trip! When Mary and I returned from New Orleans by plane, I could hardly remember back to the day we had landed at Cave-in-Rock.

: 25 :   COLORED STEAM

IN THE UPPER Mississippi River on our annual cruise to St.
Paul, Minnesota, crowds hurried for miles to watch the
Delta Queen pass through a lock. What a thrill it was to
wide-eyed children of the midwest to watch the boat all lit
up from stem to stern and top to bottom as she glided like
a floating palace into the narrow concrete lock chamber on
a moonlit evening in late September.

The captain, wearing his white uniform decorated
with gold braid and brass buttons, bellowed important orders from the bridge on top deck outside the pilot house:
"Back her, come ahead a turn; get your possum in there,
up the river a little, all fast," as the boat slowed her pace,
and was tied securely to the lock wall.

Greetings such as "Good evening, Cap, how many you
got this trip?" came from the lock master on shore.

"How are you sir? We got one hundred and ninety
this time. A full house. Nice weather we're having this
trip," Captain replied. This information as to the number
of passengers was a legal report which was made to each
lock master as we passed through the lock.

On all decks a multitude of passengers lined up at the
railing to watch the interesting on-shore activity of this
"touch and go" visit. They often tossed coins or bits of
wrapped candy to the children, who put on a refreshing
show as they scrambled and tusseled for a precious prize.
These passengers were all from far away—California, Alas-

ka, New York, or many other distant cities and states—unlike Keokuk, Iowa or Red Wing, Minnesota—and were fascinated by what they saw ashore.

After the boat was tied fast to the lock wall and while the water was in process of being raised or lowered to the level of the water ahead in the marine stairway of the upper Mississippi, the calliope at the stern of the top deck took over. First the steam was slowly spewed from its pipes, in a sort of tuning up process. Then amid shouts and loud applause the music began and a shrill medley of tunes appropriate for the occasion echoed across the countryside— "On Wisconsin," "Red Wing" or perhaps "Missouri Waltz," plus a general repertoire of other familiar melodies. At night everyone marveled at the colored steam this "steam piano" emitted during the concert. Some never quite figured how this effect was produced. Rumors could be heard of "They have colored water in the boilers," and other far fetched ideas of devices indigenous to mysterious steamboat folk could be overheard among those of the crowd who were uninformed of the scientific facts. Actually it was huge colored electric bulbs placed in outlets near the steam pipes that produced this rainbow effect, which was a delight to watch as the shrill notes blasted forth.

Grandmothers clutching the hands of small grandchildren carefully explained with pointing gestures all they knew about the big steamboat which neither had ever seen before. If the schedule was such that the boat passed through the lock during school hours, nearby schools dismissed specifically so the children could see the locking process.

The purser sometimes straddled over the railings and hurried to the phone booth ashore to dispatch an urgent message or the steward hurried to phone in an order for supplies: perhaps a case of tomatoes, and two dozen loaves of bread, or a case of eggs to be delivered at the next landing.

As soon as the boat reached the proper water level, the lines were cast off the lock wall and hauled onto the boat by the strong deck hands below. Soon farewell tunes of, "Goodbye Little Girl, Goodbye," "Smile the While I Bid You Fond Adieu," or "I'll See You in My Dreams," sounded from the calliope. The big red paddle wheel churned up a heavy wake as she cleared the lock chamber, sending waves rocking along the shore as she splashed out of sight down the river and around the bend. This mysterious phantom of another world was long remembered by everyone on shore. They shouted goodbyes and waved as long as they could see the boat and hear "The Lilt of the Calliope," a winsome tune written by our friend and stockholder E. J. Quinby especially for the Delta Queen.

The passengers waved a final farewell to this refreshing river experience and returned to resume their bridge game, to relax on deck or engage in whatever activity they enjoyed most at that moment.

One lady expressed it well: "That was truly a touch of the 'heart' of America!" she announced fervently.

: 26 :   ST. PAUL, 1965

SEPTEMBER EQUINOX storms were at a peak all over the country. In Hyde Park, Cincinnati I began to think the whole weather complex had settled here, with clouds emptying all their supply of rain at my home. Tired from lack of sleep the previous night I failed to have the proper thrilled feeling of excitement, only the realization that I was due in Louisville, Kentucky by nine a.m. with my luggage. There, I was to embark on the *Delta Queen* for a three week cruise in the upper Mississippi to St. Paul, which fell in the line of duty of the President and General Manager of Greene Line Steamers. I'd promised the Captain I'd be there.

At six-thirty on Sunday with suitcases in hand and dress bags thrown over our arms, my daughter Jane and I loaded our car in a downpour, then wearily started on the one-hundred-mile drive to the *Delta Queen*. This was not an unusual experience for me, as I have so often gone to meet the boat, or gone out on her for a short portion of a trip. It had become a duty similar to that of a bus driver picking up his route, or a train engineer joining his cab at his part of the run of an extended train schedule. These boat jaunts had been woven into my pattern of life for several years.

But this, was a record run. On old snaky narrow Route 42, it is sane to cover the distance from Cincinnati to Louisville in three hours—no less. But perhaps not many sane people were out on the road at this early hour on a rainy Sunday morning. Two and one-half hours found us driving up the gangplank of the waiting steamboat at the public landing in Louisville. After the car was safely placed on board, the Captain gonged the big bell. A long and a short whistle blew as we headed downstream to lock around the falls, through the canal.

This cruise was a sellout with very little left over space available for us "dead heads." A passenger asked me once if I kept a nice parlor reserved for my own occupancy whenever I choose to come aboard the boat. I explained how we just took what was left over, never occupying space which was needed by our customers. Sometimes, of course, this meant a deluxe parlor, for not everyone could afford the most luxurious accommodations on many trips, and the left over space could often turn out to be the best room on the boat. Not on this St. Paul cruise: the left over space was definitely just what the term connotes, "left over."

In this case the "leftover" assigned to me was a room on "skid row." A row of less desirable cubicles across the stern of the cabin deck took on this unique name. It was space which would not be attractive to paying passengers but did serve the good purpose of housing the remnants of the ship's crew that could not be accommodated in the regular officers' quarters on top deck.

A certain folksy camaraderie among these crew members made it tolerable and while the rooms were small, noisy, and often hot, the privacy they afforded in a measure compensated for other inconveniences. One could sit outside the door of the "skid row" rooms and relax in lounging apparel, being lulled to a state of near hypnotism by the churning of the water as the big red paddle wheel rhythmically lapped off her eighteen turns per minute. Under normal navigation conditions the noise of the engine room at times seemed to transpose into a percussion section of the overall river symphony.

In Room 139, one's possessions had to be placed in the compact area with efficient care, in order to utilize every corner, shelf, nail, and cranny of the walls. There was no room for unnecessary extras in this cubicle which was my domain for almost three weeks whenever I wanted to sleep or rest.

My room served a dual purpose. My oldest daughter, who was part of the entertainment department, used this space as a walk-in cupboard to store all her wardrobe. The clothing hung from a heavy lead pipe running the entire length at the ceiling level. At the head end of the bunk was the convenient arrangement of a fold-up shelf made by her husband, the assistant purser. When not in use it folded closely to the bulkhead and fastened by means of a screen door hook. While in use, it extended out from the wall and served to hold a portable sewing machine. This was in frequent use, as Mary made most of her clothes and was constantly browsing in the various towns and cities along the river where the boat docked for yard goods bargains and unusual patterns. I often told her if fabric departments were alcohol, she'd be an alcoholic.

There was, of course, a basin into which ran both hot and cold water, a window with horizontal shutters, and space under the bunk to store a small suitcase. If one could shove the dresses which hung from the ceiling lead pipe far enough toward the foot of the bed, get undressed and into just the right position, with a nice little reading light at the head of the bed it had a certain coziness where one could relax and enjoy the latest best seller. However, if Mary should happen to come to the room during my resting period to finish up a zipper seam, or sew the belt onto a skirt the feeling created by the bulkhead on three sides of the bed, the clothes in dry cleaning bags overhead and the opened shelf with the portable sewing machine on it to my left was a mild attack of claustrophobia. (So—they think I have a special room set aside for myself, do they?)

At St. Louis I went ashore and equipped myself with yarn, knitting needles and instruction books to take up my spare time when I was not talking to passengers, telling tales of the river to newcomers or just looking around to see how things were going. Much of this knitting I did in my room; in fact, I very nearly wore myself out doing this absurd thing—never closing my eyes until late, late at night. (There were, often, however, other reasons I didn't sleep.)

The passengers on this trip were the usual lot. The majority were elderly, but a few were under fifty. The cocktail lounge was not too crowded, bedtime was a popular hour with most all the travelers, and card games were a great pastime during the day and early evening. There was bingo, marine horse racing and the usual shipboard entertainment. The scenery was unexcelled anywhere on the western river system. Weather warm—not warm enough for air conditioning, but too warm to be comfortable in a completely closed room.

In order to enjoy the river breezes and yet have privacy in my room I devised a sort of "Sheik of Araby" arrangement by suspending a doubled sheet pinned over another lead pipe which ran above the door. I could then by fastening the door open, have entrance to my room by pulling aside the sheet, sneak into my tent and I'd have privacy with fresh air. This is accepted in the book of etiquette and good taste on a river boat. Informality is usually in order.

There had been rain from the time the boat left Cincinnati and it continued. Some talk of a flood—but we passed that off as only conjecture, for who had ever heard of a flood in September in the upper Mississippi? None of our older river people could recall such a condition.

The various upper river towns are nestled down near the river bank, for there is not ordinarily the danger of flood in this section of the upper river system. La Crosse, Wisconsin, was an inviting shore stop, where on Sunday morning (one week from the time I left home) all had an opportunity to attend the church of their choice. The park down near the river was filled with natives down to see us land. Hundreds of sightseers lined the banks as the *Delta Queen* eased into the landing and discharged those who felt a need for religious worship or perhaps just wanted to stretch their legs. The hospitality of these towns thrills everyone. If one hired a cab to go to church, more than likely a member of the congregation would recognize him as a stranger, strike up a short conversation and end up taking him for a ride over the town to see the sights, returning to the boat by sailing time.

When we reached St. Paul the weather was dreary, damp and the river rising. The usual stay of a day and a night gave everyone an opportunity for sightseeing via a guided bus tour of the twin cities and gave me a chance to have my car winterized, for this was pretty far north. I had planned to drive home when we returned to St. Louis.

Rain continued! Fog set in, and the boat was twelve hours late leaving St. Paul. "River Rising Fast" headlines in the local papers gave warnings of flood.

The dams in the upper Mississippi are all close together, some perhaps not over fifty miles apart. The channels in some areas are narrow, flanked on the side by jagged rocks and dangerous shoals. I much prefer going upstream into locks during flood water, for then there seems to be more control of the steering process. But coming downstream on a full river with a strong current is similar to being pushed downstairs by a strong force, knowing that just at the foot of the stairs is a narrow door and corridor through which one must pass: slowly, with care not to hit the sides of the passageway but with enough force to continue straight on and stop just short of a door at the edge of a high precipice.

The boat must have speed enough to shape up and enter the lock chamber properly, and at the same time sufficient ease not to hit the wall or bump the exit gate to the lower level. The orders given by the Captain to the pilot influence the success of this procedure greatly and these orders are sent through a P.A. system to the pilot as well as to the deck hands below, both forward and stern.

One of these loudspeakers was directly under my room, making sound, uninterrupted sleep difficult. As the boat ran head-on toward a dam, I would first hear the long and short blast of the whistle, which assured me we were coming ahead full speed toward the entrance gate of the lock chamber. Suddenly I'd hear over the loud speaker, "Stop her—STOP her!" louder and louder. At this point I'd brace my feet as I awoke from the first deep nap of the night, push hard against the bulkhead as if it were a brake. I expected the next minute to hear a crash and the shattering of glass and dishes from the pantry downstairs, and sliding deck chairs outside as the boat slammed into the concrete lock wall. At last came Captain Wagner's "All fast." Relieved, I'd return to the comforts of my bed and dream away until the whole process was repeated. St. Paul —the first flood waters in a hundred years.

One night, I was fortunate to avoid one of the exciting events of the trip. I can't imagine why.

The pilot blew for a lock; we entered the lock chamber and the boat was lowered properly. He got the come ahead signal which meant that the lift bridge at the exit end of the lock chamber was ready for the boat to come through. The *Delta Queen* came ahead at the proper speed. Someone had surely misfigured, for the smoke stack extension smacked the bridge, tore off at the joint and simply jumped backwards and sat down with the sound of a bomb on the roof behind the stationary portion of the stack, which remained intact just back of the pilot house. This brought every member of the crew out of bed instantly. Their rooms were directly underneath.

Captain Wagner leaped out in his underwear and headed for the exit gangway. Mary jumped out of her bed and lunged out the door of the room which she and her husband, the purser, occupied nearby. She and the Captain collided in the gangway too alarmed to be embarrassed. The noise was terrifying but for once I slept through it all. After discovering that no serious damage was incurred, the boat proceeded on downstream, but there were many jokes and belly laughs in the crew's dining room next day about Mary and the Captain's early morning collision on top deck.

Of course the stack had to be repaired, but we got back to St. Louis intact and on time. With a three-inch clearance at the Eads bridge, the boat landed high on the levee, almost touching high-power lines and with a rare view of that St. Louis levee. I was happy when I discovered that the high water made it impossible for my car to be driven off the boat. This had been a strenuous trip, and I didn't care to drive home. Jane and I made reservations on the first jet for Cincinnati to go home, there intending to rest from my Flood Trip of 1965, in Room 139, to St. Paul. In a matter of forty-five minutes by TWA, we sliced through the distance covered by the steamboat in four days a week or so before, returning to fair skies, sunny autumn days, approaching Indian summer with its charm of frosty mornings, and dreams of future trips to the home of Dixieland Jazz, creole mammys, pralines and Bourbon Street: New Orleans. Another close shave was over for the *Queen* in keeping her published schedule. Three-inch clearance at the Eads Bridge is just too close for comfortable steamboat navigation.

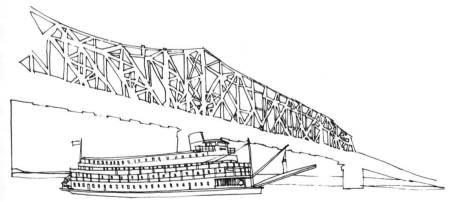

: 27 : A GUEST FOR DRY DOCK

FOR A WOMAN, life aboard a steamboat in dry dock beggars description. I had this experience for the first time in November 1930. We had been married in October of that year and came aboard the steamer *Tom Greene* to live for five years, before establishing a permanent home ashore. So I was aboard when the boat left for a repair job at the Marine Ways in Madison, Indiana. I was a bride of two months, new to river life, and certainly new to drydock life aboard a steamboat.

My mother-in-law, Captain Mary B. Greene, and I found ourselves in the unique position of being cooks for a crew of approximately fifteen men. This amazing culinary feat was accomplished on a coal range about six feet wide and three feet deep. I was not an experienced cook, but I soon learned the art of baking navy beans and weiners to perfection. All water for cooking purposes was carried in large pails from a source up the hill. One of the deck hands, "Big Nat", so called because he weighed four hundred pounds, was assigned the duty of dishwasher. We knew the kitchen would be well cleaned and tidied up following every meal.

The boat, which was pulled high and dry half-way "up the Hill", was devoid of heat, and toilet facilities were primitive. The cook house, as a kitchen is called on a steamboat, was warm from the heat of the cook stove, but only at certain times of the day. Also the texas, an area on top deck where the crew washed up, was equipped with a pot-bellied coal stove, which, if fired forcefully enough, could "run you out of the place". The texas was a small folksy spot which contained a table, a few bentwood chairs, an old pedal sewing machine, wash basins, a sink, a coal bucket, shovel and poker, a few magazines and books, and other trivial odds and ends. In the living room of our small private apartment was located a coal-burning heatrola which made that room a comfortable one in which to lounge at times. But the staterooms were cold and uncomfortable.

Two days after we were settled on dry dock, my mother-in-law received a long distance phone call at the shipyard office. She hurried up the hill, anxious to see what urgent message awaited her.

The voice came clear, "Captain Mary, this is Bertha Meecher. I'm in Cincinnati." She lived in Cleveland.

"Oh, hello Bertha. How are you?"

"I'm fine. I'm coming down to visit you," replied Bertha. She was a casual acquaintance, not an intimate friend and this announcement came as a mild shock to Captain Mary.

"Oh, we're on dry dock, you know, Bertha, up out of the water," Captain Mary hastened to explain.

"Yes, I know, but it would be such an unique experience. I shan't mind it at all. I'll be down on the five o'clock bus tomorrow."

Captain Mary ordinarily would have welcomed a guest, for she was an outgoing friendly person. But somehow this didn't seem the time or the place to entertain city friends. Still, she attempted to be gracious.

The next day Captain Mary met the bus and entertained her guest for dinner uptown at the Mountain View Hotel. This was at least a good beginning.

Each meal following this first gesture of hospitality was to be aboard the *Tom Greene* in the cook house. We served the crew first on an easily cleaned oilcloth-covered table and afterwards we covered one end of the table with a crisp white linen cloth in an attempt to make things "company" style for Mrs. Meecher. However, when her stay stretched into days and weeks, we invited her to slide in on the bench alongside the firemen, deck hands and other workmen—style be hanged. She seemed to enjoy every minute of her self-imposed river visit. Her hobby was painting roses. She carried out this occupation in the texas room seated at a card table. She painted by the hour—book covers, stationery, greeting cards, vases and mirrors were all decorated with hand-painted roses. The mate 'lowed as how, "She'd soon start in on the life preservers if a halt wasn't called on this dainty past time!"

Each Sunday carloads of river friends found it convenient and desirable to drive the sixty-five miles from Cincinnati to Madison to see the boat as she sat high and dry and to observe the repair work in progress. This meant a larger trough of beans and a greater roaster of pork chops would be prepared to serve the guests.

The weather became bitter cold and we feared for the health of our elderly guest, but there was no evidence that she had any notion of going back to warmer city quarters. Since Tom and I had business in Cincinnati one afternoon, we suggested to Mrs. Meecher that inasmuch as the weather conditions called for approaching snow storms this would be a good chance for her to return to Cincinnati and not risk further inconveniences of cold weather on the boat. We delivered her to her relatives in Cincinnati just in time: as we returned to Madison and the boat the storm hit. We were blinded by the blizzard and could bare-

ly make our way over the snow-buried Indiana road which
at that time connected Cincinnati with Madison. What a
relief to be freed of the added social responsibility of being
host to one who is not accustomed to roughing it on the
river in dry dock.

This drydock ordeal lasted a month, after which the
boat was slowly floated back into the water. This time we
headed for Gallipolis, Ohio and more repairs at the Acme
Boiler Shop, which was owned by Greene Line and operated by Charley Arthur and his family.

At Gallipolis, conditions were perhaps better. At least
we had a few less crew members to cook for. The boat was
afloat in the water, but the only means of going ashore and
up the hill was by way of a series of steps dug out of the
river's mud bank. They were deep enough to give good
footing but when freshly dug were a bit treacherous in wet
weather. Rain set in. Tom made a quick trip to buy a few
emergency items for tomorrow's breakfast. With his arms
laden with eggs, bacon, bread, coffee, sausage, onions, and
oranges for the larder, he started his descent on the freshly
dug, slippery, mud steps. You guessed it! His feet went out
from under him, eggs flew up in the air, some smashing on
his head, some plopping in the river, bread crushed into
soft dough lumps, oranges rolled over the hill, and he was
mud from head to toe. I shan't describe it further, to do so
would be sinful.

There were many bright moments at the Acme Boiler
repair shop. We had numerous friends in Gallipolis who
were more than generous with invitations to dine and visit
in their homes: the Arthur family's warm hearth, the Sib-
leys', the Halidays', and the Maddys'. We felt at home so
many places and had a good chance to visit with all our
friends. This session led up until Christmas, when we man-

aged to make it back into Cincinnati for the holidays. By now, I felt I had had a genuine first hand idea of what it's like to live on a boat in dry dock.

It was twenty-seven years later that I had a session aboard the *Delta Queen* on the Marine Ways at Dravo Shipyard, Pittsburgh, Pennsylvania. A recent Coast Guard rule decreed that every five years a steamboat should be pulled out of the water for hull inspection "whether she needed it or not." So in the autumn of 1957 we started for Dravo Shipyard. A few river buffs seemed to believe that this was a trip much to be desired and were anxious to come along. We had a goodly number of guests. A skeleton crew, the chef, the steward, and enough deck hands to fill the law were aboard as we steamed up the Ohio toward Pittsburgh.

The trip was pleasant with the fall coloring waving its somber goodbyes, but winter promised soon to be upon us. Nights and some days were cold. Again we were lifted high and dry in a mechanically incredible fashion at Dravo Shipyards. It seemed unbelievable that we could actually walk underneath the mammoth steel hull of the boat as it formed a ceiling over our head.

We were fortunate enough to find things in good shape and were able to get by with only a minimum of repairs ordered by the Coast Guard. Aboard the boat again, as is usually the case, the place was cold, dreary and bleak. Heat was generated on a unit in the shipyard and delivered to the boat by means of a long canvas tubing about two feet in diameter. This hose was somehow placed in the boat's main cabin through an opening in a window. One could feel the extreme hot blast of air if one stood directly and closely in front of the tube, but any distance away in any direction the heat became so diluted with cold air and breeze from the open cracks and crevices that the atmosphere was frigid. It seemed a better idea to wear a coat and depend on body heat in that fashion than to rely entirely on heat from the hose. Only after midnight could the toilets or basins be emptied of their contents, since there were no workers underneath the boat then, in danger of getting a sewage bath while pounding or riveting on the job.

This became a midnight ceremony on the boat. One could set his watch by the gurgling of water and the flushing of toilets in one great volley of attack after twelve o'clock. For entertainment a radio here and there blasted forth with a popular song of the year. Meals were served on time. Other than that one was on his own. Listening to triphammers and watching welding torches and cranes soon grows a bit old even if one's eyes and ears can hold out. Still, it was necessary for us to be on the job lest a decision need to be made or some papers signed, so we remained on the reservation. A long enough distance from Pittsburgh to make a trip to town for any amusement more trouble than pleasure, it seemed like a reservation.

The environment became a health hazard. Mary came down with the flu and developed a severe sore throat. I borrowed a car from one of the officers of our company, who had driven up, and we drove back to Cincinnati to restore our health and happiness. In two more days the boat was lowered into the Ohio River and started for home, after having incurred a sizeable bill which ate into our financial vitals rather heavily that year, 1957.

It was in 1962 that the *Delta Queen* was again drydocked, the last session which it was my duty to attend. Again at Dravo's—but this time I did not ride the boat up the river. Instead, my son Gordon and I drove to Pittsburgh to be there when the work started, and during its progress. I recall having knitted an entire snow suit for my infant grandson Chris Greene this time, while we awaited the welding and the hammering and the general noise of the shipyard repair work to end.

The dry docking duties became more complicated as the years went by and the demands became greater. I can speak only for those prior to 1967, at which I was in attendance. I can only comment that it was an expensive but necessary task to be done, interesting to men, maybe, who understand such carryings on. But to a woman, or at least to *this* woman, drydocking a steamboat is not the most thrilling experience imaginable. It falls in the category of defrosting a long-neglected refrigerator, weeding a garden or deticking a dog: an unpleasant task but one which is a relief to have done in good order, though it is an operation which can measurably flatten the purse.

OUT OF DEBT AND ON TO WASHINGTON

: 28 :

IN SPITE OF THE many setbacks which assailed the *Delta Queen,* her mortgage was completely cleared on October 3, 1960. This was happy cause for celebration on my thirtieth wedding anniversary. I'm sure it was a surprise to our mortgagee, who had so many times followed through on the faintest hope of a chance to sell the boat in order to clear the loan. None of these nibbles had proved to be worthwhile, and it turned out to be a better policy to hang on patiently and hopefully.

By 1962, the entire slate of indebtedness was clear and everyone was happy to have been paid in full. And by 1964, following a season of profitable business, a profit-sharing plan was set up for our employees. The company's debts were paid, and we were in a position to begin to share with those whose services had been so important to us. Things were working out well at Greene Line and at home, my children were all either through college or about to graduate.

I began to wonder how much longer I could continue to head the business, as years were a bit heavy on my shoulders. There seemed to be no one anxiously beating a path to my door to take over my responsibilities. My oldest son, Gordon, was well into his law practice and Tom Jr. well established in the commercial art field. Although Mary, my oldest had been hostess aboard the *Delta Queen* for six years and her husband had a great knowledge of the river as a crew member, they were by now established in the city and had no further river inclinations. Jane, my youngest, was at the University, preparing for a teaching profession.

Our general organization seemed more secure with very fine and reliable help. Headed by Betty Blake, our capable new publicity department was working overtime and at last, fortune seemed to be casting a favorable glance our way. By this time I had become so familiarly acquainted with hard luck and deprivation in the business that it seemed unnatural to be prosperous. Now we had even indulged in some new décor for the boat. Everyone was in a better mood.

One April afternoon I was sitting at my desk making out an order for the souvenir stand, when a long distance call from Chicago was relayed to my line. It was the President of Georgian Bay Line of the Great Lakes, a good friend, and head of a company which for years had been friendly competition in some ways. We continually exchanged ideas, and even employees when needed, and we had good rapport with the lake boats. Our problems were akin, only different in size and location.

"Hello, Letha, this is Erv Goebel. We've had word of some action of Congress which would put our boats out of business on July 1st. Have you heard about it?"

"No Erv, we have not. What's up?"

"A hearing is to be held in Washington this week. The news actually came to us in a roundabout way, not an official notice. But my attorney and I are going to Washington tomorrow."

This was the first pronouncement I had of what

turned out to be a fateful moment for the *Delta Queen*. Out of business! Would she die again? And on such short notice.

This telephone conversation was comparable to "the shot heard around the world," in river circles. Long distance calls that month piled up on the Greene Line bill. I often wondered what would have happened if we hadn't had this unofficial information in this strange way. It is sometimes difficult to understand the working of our "establishment", as it is known today in some circles.

My son, Gordon, who was an officer of our company, and I took the next plane for Washington, there to join West Coast and East Coast Greene Line officials, the Georgian Bay Line men and to meet with the congressional committee. Many other steamship companies were present at the hearing because of the Safety-at-Sea Law, arguing for their right to exist.

The Madison Hotel was our meeting place to lay our planned attack the day prior to the hearing. After a dinner in the elegant hotel dining room, we retired to our quarters to discuss all angles of our problems, until well into the morning hours. It was upon this occasion that I met a gentleman who was in the not-too-far-away future to become president of Greene Line and play a vastly important role in her future: Mr. William Muster. He was a representative of Mr. Simonton's West Coast Muzak business and accompanied Dick on this occasion to see what he could do to help out in our dilemma. Chairman of the board E. J. Quinby did an eloquent job of presenting our case before the Congressional committee.

The official business was all so new to me, interesting, yet confusing. I could never see why the *Delta Queen,* a mere riverboat, should be included in the Safety-at-Sea Law, which was intended for ocean vessels. We were not thousands of miles away from land at any time, and it didn't seem reasonable. Since there were ideas of building a replacement for the *Delta Queen,* though, maybe things would work in our favor. My idea of making an appeal for exemption from the law was overruled and the next chapter in the Queen's life began!

Mr. Muster came to the fore with great influence and capability. Greene Line soon underwent some vast changes, and I realized it was beyond my power to fight this congressional battle. Time for me to exit gracefully and gladly.

On the day that I stepped aside to allow the younger and more efficient generation to take over the wheels of industry, the *Delta Queen's* paddle wheel to be specific, my son Gordon remarked "Mom, today I believe we have witnessed the changing of the watch." I was glad! At least now someone could start in with fresh new blood, and I could stand by and watch the show.

Mr. Muster was starting out now in a new ball game. I wondered if he would learn by experience trying many things which we had cast off as impractical years before. You can't change "old man river" and his people, he's bigger than all of us!

: 29 : HILO AIRPORT

Rain fell in monsoon proportions at the airport in Hilo, Hawaii that November night in 1969, as we wearily awaited our eleven p.m. United Airlines flight for Los Angeles. The baby slept in his father's arms as we sat watching the milling crowd which would soon be whisked through the wet black night to the U.S. mainland or other faraway destinations. It had been a full two weeks for my daughter Mary, her husband Richard Stewart, their son Joel and me. A steep hike in the afternoon to Akaka Falls, a final touch to our island activities, was more strenuous than I had anticipated, and a ten hour flight faced us back to Cincinnati and home.

The anxiously awaited sale of *Delta Queen* stock to Over Seas National Airways of New York had been brewing for months. There were conferences, followed by lengthy legal contracts and documents which fattened my files. Gordon, Caroline and family had hesitated to venture their trip to Europe and the Greek Isles last June lest the final settlement date slip by during their leave, but arrangements were made, everyone's plans went on uninterrupted, and here I was, so many miles away from home in November still wondering how the deal was progressing. I was startled by a loud announcement, "Letha Greene, calling Letha Greene." My name!

"What can be wrong with my ticket?" I was startled back to consciousness. It was only a half hour before flight time, and I hurried to the ticket desk.

167

"You are to call Cincinnati; here is the number." The polite young Japanese clerk handed me a note: my son Gordon's telephone number.

I had talked with him only two days before, and surely there was no business so urgent that I should be called at this hour—it was three a.m. in Cincinnati. Messages of this nature still jolt me, a kickback, I suppose to days of my childhood when a telegram or long distance call meant bad news. This message was not so bad.

Soon a half awake son in Indian Hill, Cincinnati, answered, "Mother, you're to send a telegram to Over Seas National Airways so it will reach their office by nine o'clock tomorrow morning. Here's what to say." He dictated a legal resignation of my present official capacity with Greene Line Steamers—a detail which was important toward closing the sale, before checks would be forthcoming.

There was no Western Union desk in the small Hilo airport, so the message had to be phoned in, and time was slipping by too fast.

"Gordon," I suggested. "I've got to get out of here. You send the message, and sign my name."

"No, Mother, if that plane dropped in the ocean tonight, my face would be red, I fear." What a comforting thought. "Get it off there, it won't take long."

After succeeding in convincing the operator that my credit card was good for telegraph purposes and trying to impress her with the importance of especially fast service in my case, she finally took the message and in a slightly Oriental accent slowly read it back to me. Oh, if she'd only hurry!

They were calling my flight. Mary appeared, rushed up and exclaimed, "Mother they're closing the doors in three minutes." I hurried out of the phone booth, after giving a quick last glance to make sure I hadn't left my billfold, credit card, pills or something else important. I ran the whole length of the concourse, where, at the gate, a steward waited for me with a huge "airplane" sized umbrella, which soon collapsed in a wet heap around my shoulders. I splashed my way to the plane, scrambled aboard and sank dripping wet into my assigned seat, exhausted. Off for the mainland on this black rainy night. I'd severed all connections with my river life and suppose the plane did drop in the ocean—it seemed somehow dramatically appropriate for me at that moment.

The door clobbered shut. Then an announcement of: "Ladies and Gentlemen, we are about to depart for Los Angeles. (And so on, and so on . . .) "

The cute, flip little Hawaiian steward added, "We hope."

I settled back, placed the ear phones to my head and turned to soft music.

SENTIMENTAL INVESTMENT

THE *Delta Queen* has won a congressional victory which permits her to continue passenger service today. I am glad I could help to span the period of time from my husband's management of the boat to the era where others can carry on the steamboat passenger service to future generations. I am sure Tom Greene would be happy to know there are those of another generation who are putting forth a valiant effort to perpetuate passenger service on western rivers today with his *Delta Queen*.

The older slower mode of travel has now become a subsidiary of the fastest mode of travel. Perhaps the old had to be given assurance by the new. The airplane has extended a kind hand and explained, "Come on steamboat, there's room for us all in today's world. We'll fly them there fast, and you take it slow and preserve the romantic way of life so typical of your age. Maybe we can bridge the generation gap."

Many will yet be able to enjoy the pleasures of a river cruise and experience the thrill of a balmy moonlight night on peaceful river waters, the hypnotic swish of the paddle wheel, and the beauty of color splashed sunsets, when the air is heavy with silence. Many have made great sacrifices toward the perpetuation of this indescribable mode of steamboat river travel. In this age of air pollution and ecology consciousness, when people seem to be seeking a way of life that is suitable to all, a river cruise should help one to sift values and allow them to fall into proper perspective. A week or more on the river is great therapy for both body and mind.

Since my exit from ownership of the boat, I still have a heavy sentimental investment as a result of my forty years association with the *Delta Queen,* and her various predecessors in the Greene Line fleet.

The phone rang. I hurried from my flower garden to answer it in the kitchen. The dog dashed out, the cat strolled in; I picked up the receiver with earth-crusted trowel in my hand.

My son, Tom, spoke out in a quizzical tone, "Mother, are you going down to see the boat come in tomorrow?"

"No, Tom, I don't think I'll be able to park on the levee with all the crowd that's expected. It's too far to park at the top of the hill and walk down with my bum knee," I replied.

"I don't think I'll make it either. Have a lot of work at the studio to get out, and had better not take the time."

"There'll be plenty of opportunities to see her later when it's not so crowded," I assured him.

Thus the conversation went between my son, Tom Jr. and me the day before the *Delta Queen* was scheduled to dock at the Cincinnati Levee, April 29, 1971: the date of her victorious homecoming.

He and I had been the only members of the Greene family who were able to see her off on what was thought to be her last trip eight months ago, and neither of us had known the other was there, I aboard the boat, and he, during his lunch hour, watching from a distance at the top of hill.

*   *   *

Today the morning was grey and cold, and the daylight saving time made eight-thirty seem too early. I donned my coat and scarf and walked out with purse in hand. I thought "I'll go and if the crowd seems to be a problem I can turn around and come home." The urge was that strong and I followed the long line of early traffic down Columbia Parkway toward the city and on to the river. I'd forgotten how hectic that hour can be with cars weaving in and out of traffic and changing lanes without warning. When I finally turned down Broadway Street toward the river the traffic was bumper to bumper.

I thought: I'll just work my way over into the left lane here, and cut over the bridge into Kentucky where I can get a perfect view from the south shore of the river. Somewhere above Mike Fink's riverboat restaurant, I found a half-way parking spot, and looked out just in time to see the *Delta Queen* easing under the Suspension Bridge. Like a new bride in her all-white garb, she slowly glided with great dignity on up the river, with her great entourage of small white pleasure boats like bridesmaids escorting her into her home port. Three sonorous blasts of her whistle echoed from the Ohio to the Kentucky hills, as the mighty red paddle wheel slowed its pace, and her bow turned toward the Ohio shore. There followed great fanfare, bands, gun salutes, with the levee alive with the human race, buses disgorging countless mobs of school children: all down to welcome the Queen home. Men and women carrying babies hurried on foot on both sides of the river to get a look from a distance at the homecoming festivities.

My mind flashed back to a Sunday in July 1947, when the *Delta Queen* entered the harbor with less glamour and almost no fanfare, when she had her first look at Cincinnati after a long adventuresome trip from faraway California. She was headed for a quarter of a century of turbulent life, and the making of river history. She was at that time reborn for the first time and was christened with conjectures such as: "Well, she's surely a monstrosity. Do you think we can make any money with her?"

"She runs smooth all right, and what freeboard! She ought to trump any ace the Old Mississippi River can play against her in a storm."

"She'll have to have a hell of a lot of remodeling to operate in this country."

"How can she ever get through the locks with the decks riding up so high?"

"Dam, she's smokin' like a smudge pot, and only one stack. Better look out for the smoke inspector. She's surely not like the boats we're used to."

"The woodwork is pretty, though, and look at all that stained glass over the windows!"

"Wonder how she handles . . ."

"Fraid she'll be a white elephant on their hands."

On and on.

Tom, my husband, was brave and unblemished by any comments which may have reached his ears. He had the boat he wanted, and now he would feel secure in any storm. This was the *Delta Queen*. *His* Delta Queen was steaming into port—alive again and ready to go. Surely he heard the calliope as she played, "Down on the Ohio."

Later that night, I dialed my son's number. "Say, Tom, I went down to see the boat come in after all!"

A loud laugh from the other end of the line: "You did? So did I. I had no trouble getting down there about 9:15—parked and watched the whole thing. She looked pretty, didn't she?"

"Well, I got in the lane going to Kentucky and watched from Covington. It was a thrilling sight to see her coming back to life again, almost unbelievable."

"And Mom, guess who I saw, one of our former passengers hurrying along in the crowd. I'll have to think of her name—you'll know her, though. Oh, she met her husband on the boat. I'll think of it soon."

Yes, I knew her all right, and I'm sure she and thousands of others all over the country rejoiced with us to know the *Delta Queen* was saved for the fifth time. And I know all will join me in a salute, "Long live the Queen!— Delta, that is."